Augie

Don,

thanks. I like you!

Greg Colon.

Acknowledgments

This book is a long time coming. I want to first thank my parents, Mary and Joseph Colosi for always encouraging me. I always heard praise from them, never a word of discouragement. I'd like to thank my partner and wife Andrea for being who she is. I'd like to thank my supporting three brothers, Gary, Mark, Mike and my sister Julie. My son Ryan taught me the lesson of keeping my word and to my daughter Courtney who gave me the excuse to write all these QuoteLessons while she was in college.

Go to FamousLifeQuotes.org to get Greg's new QuotesLessons delivered to your email box.

Published by Colosi Family Publishing

II

Forward

So, it's the first week of classes of my undergraduate degree. Dad says that he is going to send me a little money to help get me through college and I should receive it every Thursday. So I rush to the mailbox to get my cash and there is this letter with the money that I wasn't expecting. I was so excited to get the money from Daddy and I'm thinking, "What the heck is this letter doing in here?" So after safely putting away the money I read the letter, which turned out to be (what my Dad calls) a QuoteLesson.

Week after week the QuoteLessons would come. He never missed a week. It ended up being QuoteLesson story time every Thursday in my dorm. All of my roommates would wait for Thursday's mail to come and I would read the QuoteLesson to them. And believe it or not, they would listen attentively. They even told me that I couldn't read it unless everyone was present. I thought, "They must really like my Dad's QuoteLessons."

The college I attended was out of town and it was good to get a little bit of home each week. And it was great to get the QuoteLesson and think about how it could come into play in our lives, or how it might have already come into play. During all of this, I never mentioned to my Dad that I was getting the QuoteLessons with the money (and I later found out that he was prepared to wait the four years I was in college before bringing it up). It wasn't until he came to visit one year that one of my roommates mentioned it to him and told him what we would do each Thursday.

Throughout the four years of college, every Thursday, like clockwork I would receive my QuoteLesson. It was great to hear some of the stories that my Dad had done over the years, the things he had heard, the mistakes he had made and suggestions for the future.

As you read through this book, think about how each individual QuoteLesson relates to your life and the people around you.

Thanks Dad! Love you!

Your Daughter,

Courtney

Contents

7

"Always Think In Terms Of WhatThe Other Person Wants."

- James Van Fleet -

8

"Character Develops Itself In The Stream Of Life."

-Johann Wolfgang Von Goelle -

9

"Determination And Perseverance Move
The World; Thinking That Others Will Do
It For You Is A Sure Way To Fail."

- Marva Collins -

10

"Don't Cry Because It Is Over---Smile Because It Happened."

- Anonymous -

11

"Human Nature Seems To Endow People With The Ability
To Size Up Everybody But Themselves."

- Unknown -

12

"I Have Learned That Success Is To Be Measured
Not So Much by The Position That One Has
Reached In Life As By The Obstacles Which
He Has Overcome While Trying To Succeed."

- Booker T. Washington -

13

"I Write When I'm Inspired, And I See To It That I'm
Inspired At Nine O'Clock Every Morning."

- Peter de Vries, Writer (1910-1993) -

14

"In The Context Of Life's Circumstances, You Can Either Be The Victim . . . Or The Victor. The Choice Is Yours."

- Barbara Thompson -

15

"Joy Comes From Using Your Potential."

- Will Schultz -

16

"Let Your Advance Worrying Become Advance Thinking And Planning."

- Winston Churchill -

17

"Nobody Can Give You Wiser Advice Than Yourself."

- Cicero -

18

"Overcoming The Unexpected And Discovering The Unknown Is What Ignites Our Spirit. It Is What Life Is All About."

- Daniel S. Goldin, NASA Administrator -

19

"Sooner Or Later Everyone Sits Down To A Banquet Of Consequences."

- Robert Louis Stevenson -

20

"Sow An Act...Reap Habit;
Sow A Habit...Reap A Character;
Sow A Character...Reap A Destiny."

- George Dana Boardman -

21

"The Greatest Weakness Of Most Humans Is Their Hesitancy To Tell Others How Much They Love Them While They're Still Alive."

- O.A.Battista -

22

"Failure is the seed of success. You must have setbacks and failure if you're ever going to make it in this world. Talk to anybody who's successful and they'll tell you about the road blocks in their life."

- Anonymous -

23

"Failure is the seed of success. You must have setbacks and failure if you're ever going to make it in this world. Talk to anybody who's successful and they'll tell you about the road blocks in their life."

- Unkown -

24

"The More Reasons You Have For Achieving Your Goal, The More Determined You Will Become."

- Brian Tracy -

25

"We Act As Though Comfort And Luxury Were The Chief Requirements Of Life, When All That We Need To Make Us Really Happy Is Something To Be Enthusiastic About."

- Charles Kingsley -

26

"We Don't Receive Wisdom; We Must Discover It For Ourselves After A Journey That No One Can Take For Us Or Spare Us."

- Marcel Proust -

27
"Work Like You Don't Need The Money, Love Like You've Never Been Hurt And Dance Like You Do When Nobody's Watching."

- Anonymous -

28
"Your outer world tends to be a reflection of your inner world."

- Brian Tracy -

29
"All Things Are Difficult Before They Are Easy."

- Thomas Fuller -

30
"As I Grow Older, I Pay Less Attention To What Men Say. I Just Watch What They Do."

- Andrew Carnegie -

31
"Do As Much As You Can, For As Many As You Can, As Fast As You Can And Someday Someone May Do Something Nice For You."

- Hugh Rundle -

32
"Judging Others Is Ignorance."

- Gregory J. Colosi -

33
"In The Middle Of Difficulty Lies Opportunity."

- Albert Einstein -

34
"Measure Your Wealth By What You'd Have Left If You Lost All Your Money."

- H. Jackson Brown -

35
"Nothing Is Impossible To A Willing Heart."
- John Haywood -

36
"There is nothing stronger than love."
- Anonymous -

37
"The great end in life is not knowledge, but action."
- Thomas Henry Huxley -

38
"The biggest risk in life you can take is taking no risks."
- Unkown -

39
"There Are People Who Have Every Reason In The World To Be Happy Who Aren't. There Are People With Genuine Problems Who Are. The Key To Happiness Is The Decision To Be Happy!
- Marianne Williamson -

40
"Those Who Help Are Helped."
- Fortune Cookie -

41
"Think you can, think you can't, either way you are right."
- Henry Ford -

42
"Most People See What Is, And Never See What Can Be."
- Albert Einstein -

43

"She who would accomplish little must sacrifice little; she who would achieve much must sacrifice much."

- James Allen -

44

"To Believe Your Own Thoughts, That Is Genius."

- Ralph Waldo Emerson -

45

"To The World You May Be One Person, But To One Person You May Be The World."

- Anonymous -

46

"We will either find a way or make one."

- Hannibal-Carthaginian General -

47

"No one is useless in the world who lightens the burden of it to anyone else."

- Charles Dickens -

48

"First ask yourself: What is the worst that can happen? Then prepare to accept it. Then proceed to improve on the worst."

- Dale Carnegie -

49

"You Are Positive, Creative And Happy To The Degree To Which You Eliminate Negative Emotions From Your Life."

- Brian Tracy -

50

"You can't fight love."

- Reinhardt Brucker -

51

"A friend can tell you things you don't want to tell yourself."

- Frances Ward Weller -

52

"A Friend Is One Who Sees Through You And Still Enjoys The View."

- Wilma Askinas, Writer -

53

"Always Think In Terms Of What The Other Person Wants."

- James Van Fleet -

54

"Determination And Perseverance Move The World; Thinking That Others Will Do It For You Is A Sure Way To Fail."

- Marva Collins -

55

"Use Every Letter You Write, Every Conversation You Have, Every Meeting You Attend To Express Your Fundamental Beliefs And Dreams. Affirm To Others The Vision Of The World You Want. You Are A Free, Immensely Powerful Source Of Life & Goodness. Affirm It! Spread It! Radiate It! Think Day And Night About It. And You Will See A Miracle Happen...The Greatness Of Your Own Life!"

- Author Unknown -

56

"To Me Success Can Only Be Achieved Through Repeated Failure and Introspection. In Fact, Success Represents 1% Of Your Work That Results From The 99% That Is Called Failure."

-Soichiro Honda, Founder, Honda Corporation -

57

"Be Thankful For All Your Blessings.
An Appreciative Person Makes A Pleasant
And Optimistic Person."

- Brian Tracy -

58

"The Most Basic Of All Human Needs Is The Need To Understand And Be Understood. The Best Way To Understand People Is To Listen To Them."

- Ralph Nichols -

59

"When An Old Person Dies, A Library Is Lost."

- Tommy Swann -

60

"I take nothing for granted. I now
have only good days, or great days."

- Lance Armstrong -

61

"There is no revenge so complete as forgiveness."

- Anonymous -

62

"In Nature There Are Neither Rewards Nor Punishment--There Are Consequences."

- Robert G. Ingersoll -

63
"You Cannot Do A Kindness Too Soon, For You Never Know How Soon It Will Be Too Late"
– Ralph Waldo Emerson -

64
"Give your best to others and don't be surprised w hen they give their best back to you."
- Jimmy D. Brown -

65
"Educated People Never Graduate."
- Bumper Sticker -

66
"He who is good at excuses is generally good for nothing else."
- Samuel Foote -

67
"An ounce of action is worth a ton of theory."
- Friedrich Engels -

68
"Life Promises Us Sorrow. It's Up To Us To Create The Joy."
- Opti the Mystic -

69
"In Nature There Are Neither Rewards Nor Punishment--There Are Consequences."
- Robert G. Ingersoll -

70
"When you blame others, you give up your power to change."
- Robert Anthony, Educator -

71

"The greatest obstacle to discovery is not ignorance --it is the illusion of knowledge."

- Daniel J. Boorstin -

72

"In Youth We Learn, In Age We Understand."

- Marie von Edner-Eschenbach -

73

"Never Take The Advice Of Someone Who Has Not Had Your Kind Of Trouble."

- Sidney J. Harris -

74

"If You're Never Scared Or Embarrassed Or Hurt, It Means You Never Take Any Chances."

- Julia Sorel -

75

"The Most Important Thing in Life is to See to it That You are Never Beaten."

- Andre Malraux -

76

"Kindness is more important than wisdom, and the recognition of this is the beginning of wisdom."

- Theodore Issac Rubin -

77

"The Purpose Of Life Is To Fight Maturity."

- Dick Werthimer -

78

"Happiness consists not in having much, but in being content with little."

- Anonymous -

79

"[Have You Ever Had] The Kind Of Morning That Lasts All Afternoon."

- John Mayer, from his song "Why Georgia" -

80

"Everybody thinks of changing humanity, but nobody thinks of changing himself."

- Leo Tolstoy -

81

"It is the reaching out with love to help another which is important....not the results. Reach out with love...that's all you need to do."

- Excerpted From A Course In Miracles -

82

"Every person born in this world represents something new, something that never existed before, something original and unique"

- Martin Buber (1878-1965) -

83

"Keep True To The Dreams Of Thy Youth"

- Johann von Schiller -

84

"By the time a man realizes that maybe his father was right, he usually has a son who thinks he's wrong. "

- Charles Wadsworth -

85
"Life may not be the party we hoped for, but while we are here we might as well dance."
- Anonymous 83 year-old woman -

86
"Life Is What Happens To You While You're Busy Making Other Plans"
- John Lenin, "Beautiful Boy" -

87
"If you act out of love, you'll always make the right decision."
- Gregory J. Colosi -

88
"Facing it, always facing it, that is the way to get through. Face it."
- Joseph Conrad -

89
The front page has nothing but man's failures."
- Earl Warren -

90
"When People Talk, Listen Completely. Most People Never Listen."
- Ernest Hemingway -

91
"If I had to live my life again, I'd make the same mistakes, only sooner."
- Tallulah Bankhead -

92

"Life is not measured by the number of breaths we take, but by the moments that take our breath away."

- Anonymous -

93

"Others are merely mirrors of you. You cannot love or hate something about another person unless it reflects to you something you love or hate about yourself."

- Anonymous -

94

"There Is More Credit And Satisfaction In Being A First-Rate Truck Driver Than A Tenth-Rate Executive."

- B.C. Forbes -

95

"Commit A Random Act Of Kindness."

- Bumper Sticker -

96

"Every Good Thought You Think Is Contributing Its Share To The Ultimate Result Of Your Life."

- Grenville Kleiser -

97

"Don't be too timid and squeamish about your actions. All life is an experiment."

- Ralph Waldo Emerson -

98

"Life is not important except in the impact it has on other lives."

- Jackie Robinson -

99

"Do Definite Good; First Of All To Yourself, Then To Definite Persons."

- John Lancaster Spalding -

100

"Be Happy For This Moment. This Moment Is Your Life."

- from the movie Unfaithful -

Preface

Hi, my name is Greg Colosi.

Like you, I'm passionate about famous life quotes. I realized early in my life that sometimes I would get more out of a quote than I would out of reading a 200-page book. I discovered inspirational books, found lots of quotes and I even had calendars with the quote-of-the-day over the years.

Since then I've been an avid collector of famous life quotes. I have a section in my day planner to write down all the famous quotes I stumble upon in my everyday travels.

Some of my life quotes have come from bumper stickers, fortune cookies, movies, newspapers, magazines, and books and most importantly, from people I know--even children.

When the Internet started, I subscribed to a bunch of the "quote-of-the-day" sites. First thing in the morning, I'd check out the newest quote of the day emails for a quote or two that I could add to my list.

I've build up a quite a list of famous quotes since I started collecting them over 36 years ago. I even supply a famous life quote of the day for my Starbucks to display at the barista counter in my little village of Pittsford, NY.

I want this book to be a new source of quotes for you. And if you'd like, you can subscribe to my website, FamousLifeQuotes.org to get my quote of the day each and every day.

As a special bonus, I will email you one of my QuoteLessons every Friday. I take a famous quote and write a 2-300-word lesson to go along with it. It all started when my daughter Courtney started college and I wanted to share some of my life lessons with her.

I wrote a QuoteLesson each week and sent it to her. She never said a word to me for 13 weeks. I didn't think she was interested in them. Come to find out, all her dorm mates would gather every Thursday and Courtney would read the QuoteLesson of the week to all of them.

I hope you get as much as I do from these famous life quotes.

When you subscribe to FamousLifeQuotes.org look for your quote of the day in your mailbox every day and your QuoteLesson on Friday's.

Make it a great day,

Greg Colosi

1

"Mom, when you are dancing and your ballet shoe comes untied, don't stop to tie it, just smile and keep on dancing."

- My niece Delaney Rose McNiece, 4-years-old -

Delaney is my niece. She is such a bundle of joy and enthusiasm. She hit it right on the nose with this quote of hers. Her teacher taught her that when you run into a roadblock in your life, just smile and keep on going. Kids instinctively know this. It's us adults that start to train them otherwise.

Start to think like a kid again. It's OK! Children have such great attitudes. We must get back to our childhood and start thinking like that again. When we were real little, we didn't even know what failure was. Do you remember falling when you first started walking? I didn't. Do you remember taking your first ride on your bike? Did you ever entertain the thought that you wouldn't learn how to ride your bike? Never! You just smiled and kept on trying, didn't you?

Setbacks, roadblocks and failure are a part of life. What kind of a life would it be if you never failed? I think it would be boring. Setbacks build character. It shows us what we're made of. It shows us how much we can grow. I don't know about you, but I learn a ton more with my "so-called failures" than I do with my successes. My biggest success in my life (business wise) was a failure. I learned the most from that experience about business and about life.

Welcome roadblocks--they are the steps to success in your life. When things don't go right, keep your head high, smile and keep dancing. I love you Delaney!

2

"My father didn't tell me how to live; he lived, and let me watch him do it."

- Clarence B. Kelland -

This really sums up my Dad's way of teaching all of his children the lessons of life. He was a parent who led by example. He didn't say, —"do as I say, not as I do"—he wasn't that kind of person. My Dad led by example and example only.

My brother Michael asked me a short time ago my theory of raising children. I guess he had a discussion with some of his friends on what was the best way to raise children. I told him that our parents raised us based on their example. He smiled and agreed.

I can only remember praise from my parents. I never heard, "You can't do this or you can't do that." I only heard positive encouragement. I only heard that it was possible to do or be anything you desired.

My Dad opened us up to all the possibilities of life. I remember the Christmas that "Santa" brought us all downhill skis. We all learned to ski and so did about a dozen of our friends because the Colosi's had skis. The same thing happened with golf. Johnny B. says that he wouldn't be into golf if it weren't for my Dad.

My Dad taught me to live now and not wait until you retire. He played golf several times a week and he took his share of golf and Vegas trips with the boys. He started spending winters in Florida in his fifties and recently in Scottsdale, living in a beautiful condo on the 9th hole at the TPC Desert course.

My Dad taught me how to be fair. He'd have one of us cut the cake and the other pick out the piece he wanted. He conducted his business like that too.

My Dad was not a man of many words; he was a man who expressed himself through his actions. You could always count on my Dad, no matter what. He was always there to help.

I will miss him. I know he's with me all the time. I know that if I need his advice, he'll still be there to share it with me. He just happens to get smarter as I get older.

I picked the right father. And I know his wisdom will guide me into the man he wants me to be. I love you Dad.

3

"A friend can tell you things you don't want to tell yourself."

- Frances Ward Weller -

A friend who can tell you things you can't tell yourself is a real, true friend. Hold on to him or her. It takes guts to tell you those things. Your friend is risking his friendship to help you.

My brother was asked by his best friend to be his best man in his wedding. My brother refused. He told him that if he was going to marry her, he would not. Today, Johnny is married to another woman-his soul mate- and has two beautiful girls. Twenty-five years later, they are still best friends. We all knew that the woman he was going to marry was not the right one for him. My brother was the only one who had the guts to tell him. And he was the only one.

4

"What the mind of man can conceive and believe, it can achieve."

- Napoleon Hill -

And this goes for you ladies too. If you can think it and believe it, it's a reality! Everything starts as a thought. Think about it. Your first job was first a thought in your head. Then you believed that thought. And then that thought became a reality when you started your job.

It's happened to you thousands of times. Maybe, sometimes, it wasn't the most positive thing that happened to you. You know how to do it though. You must take those positive things you want to happen in your life and muster them up.

You can't think them up unless they are possible. Your brain wouldn't let that happen. So, maybe you dismiss them because you don't think they are possible. You're wrong! They are possible. You thought them up. Now that we've got that settled, make it happen. You thought it up. Believe it now. Now it's a reality.

"A Friend Is One Who Sees Through You And Still Enjoys The View."

- Wilma Askinas, Writer -

If you can leave this life with one or two people in your life that you can call a real friend, you've done well.

I learned a lesson early in my business career. I took a very successful business owner out for lunch a dozen or so times over the course of a two-year period. He was my business mentor at the time. We decided to do some business. He told me to contact his Vice President of Sales. I called him and told him that "my friend" (the mentor) suggested that I call him. We met and did some business.

Next time I had lunch with my mentor he gave me a lesson about what friendship is that I've never forgot. He explained to me what a friend was and that .I was not his friend. I was his acquaintance and someone he was helping out.

Friends, he told me were together through thick and thin for a long time. A friend is someone who calls you and sees you more when times are tough. A friend does not take advantage of you. A friend does not get jealous of you becoming successful and being happy. A friend does not talk behind your back. A friend knows every little secret about you and doesn't use it against you. You can call a really good friend and know before you call that they will do whatever it is you're asking---and they will do it out of love.

So every time the "friend" word is used, I remember Gene. Thank you for the lesson and God rest your soul.

6

"A Truly Great Person Is The One Who Gives You A Chance."

- Paul Duffy -

Has anybody ever given you a chance? What did that do for your self-esteem? Give back. Do you have the opportunity to give someone a chance? If you do, take a chance on someone. They might just surprise you.

I've been fortunate enough to be able to give people a chance. I picked the people that no one else wanted because of their lack of education, job skills, the way they looked and various other reasons.

They were the best of the crowd. Most of them cherished the opportunity to prove themselves. And most of them did things only I knew they could do---now they know they can do them too.

You've got to go out on a limb, trust your instincts and give your fellow human beings a chance. They will rise to the occasion and make it happen for you and most importantly, for themselves.

I have letters from a few of them telling me of their journeys in life. They are some of my most prized possessions.

When you give others a chance, you are giving yourself a chance to spread your love and kindness---and that's what it's all about!

7

"Always Think In Terms Of What The Other Person Wants."

- James Van Fleet -

Your first consideration should be how this "next act of yours" will affect the other person. The other person could be your spouse, your kids, your parents, your friends, your co-workers or someone you just met.

How will your friend react to what you are about to do? Always keep their feelings in mind. Always be considerate. Being considerate is one of the finest characteristics you can have as a human being. Being thoughtful is such a nice quality.

Think about your friends and family: are they thoughtful, considerate, selfless and giving? The ones that are like this are the ones you like the most---right? Take those qualities and model yourself after them. Notice how they react to certain situations and you do the same.

Opening the door, letting someone in line first at the supermarket, letting someone in traffic or just being nice and friendly is thinking of someone else before you. If you make a habit of doing this, your life will be full of joy and love---I promise!

8

"Character Develops Itself In The Stream Of Life."

-Johann Wolfgang Von Goelle -

Who you are is your character. Do you do what you say you're going to do---even though you might not want to do it?

When my son was 7 years old, he taught me a character lesson. He said: "Dad, sometimes we don't do what you say we're gonna do." I said, "What do you mean?" He said, "You said we were going to see Teenage Ninja Turtles movie last week and we didn't." He also informed me of some other times I didn't follow through. It's been 14 years, and, not once did I not do what I told him we were going to do.

That lesson has infiltrated into all areas of my life. I don't say I'm gonna call someone for lunch if I don't ever have that intention. I don't say, "Let's get together sometime," if I don't mean it.

This is only one area of character---thank you Ryan for teaching me this one. I love you.

9

"Determination And Perseverance Move The World; Thinking That Others Will Do It For You Is A Sure Way To Fail."

- Marva Collins -

You and only you will make it happen for you. Don't count on anyone else. You have your best interests in mind, nobody else does.

When you are young you have a tendency to wait for others to help you make things happen in your life. IT DOESN'T WORK LIKE THAT! If you want your life to go in a certain direction---you must step out of the pack and make it a reality.

You can do it! You have what it takes get out of life exactly what you want. There are people that will guide you, but not do it for you. Use them. They are all around you. You must seek them out. Sometimes they are hidden in books. Sometimes they'll cross your path exactly when you need them.

They are called teachers or mentors. When you are ready to learn the teacher will appear. You must recognize him or her though.And don't ever waste your teacher's lesson. If you waste your lesson, it is less likely that another teacher will show up next time when you need him.

You have been equipped with everything you need to make your life into whatever you want. You have determination. You have perseverance. You have the ability to never give up until you reach your goals.

Don't count on anybody but yourself to build your life. Nobody will come to your rescue. Nobody will be concerned about you like you will. I know you can do it. You do too.

10

"Don't Cry Because It Is Over---
Smile Because It Happened."

- Anonymous -

It did happen. Be grateful for the time it was happening. It was a positive experience for you or you wouldn't be crying when it was over. You were into it while it was going on in your life. So that time wasn't wasted. It was a positive experience.

Maybe it was a relationship that made you cry when it was over. The other person (I'm sure) cried too. Did you have a great time together? Did you learn anything? Was she/he a good person? I'm sure the answer to all of those is "yes." If that was the case---SMILE!!

Smile because you had great time. Smile because you learned something. Smile because you met and now know a good person.

If when you think of that person, it makes you smile, it was a great relationship, even though it ended. Life brought you that person for a reason. Maybe it's not clear now---it will be one day.

Smile for all the love and people you have in your life. Keep smiling and more will be attracted to you. Try putting a little love into everything you do and watch the smiles come.

11

"Human Nature Seems To Endow People With The Ability To Size Up Everybody But Themselves."

- Unknown -

Why is this? Why do we look at other people and say this and that about them? It's very hard not to. You have to make a conscious effort not to. It's very difficult.

Guess what? We're sizing up that part of them that we don't like about ourselves. We wouldn't size it up if we were comfortable with it.

What right do you have to look someone over? You and I don't. What would you say about yourself if you saw you out in public? You and I don't have the right to judge someone. That is not our right.

Try this: next time you're out and you start to judge---judge them in a positive way. Something like: "She looks like a very nice person." "What a good father he looks like." "She seems so sweet." "What a great attitude." Try substituting statements like these instead of the other internal talking you might have been doing.

One of the side benefits is that you'll start to take it easy on yourself. You shouldn't judge yourself either. That's a whole other quote lesson.

"I Have Learned That Success Is To Be Measured Not So Much by The Position That One Has Reached In Life As By The Obstacles Which He Has Overcome While Trying To Succeed."

- Booker T. Washington -

You talk to anyone who you consider successful and he'll tell you about all the setbacks he had. Obstacles are a part of success. Without obstacles, there is no success. Be prepared to overcome many, many setbacks and obstacles on your journey to success.

If there were no obstacles, everyone would be successful. Those obstacles were put there to determine the amount of persistence and belief you have in yourself. What you overcome determines the staying power and belief you have in yourself.

So know that when those tough, unbearable situations come along—they are there for a purpose—to help you become successful!

13

"I Write When I'm Inspired, And I See To It That I'm Inspired At Nine O'Clock Every Morning."

- Peter de Vries, Writer (1910-1993) -

You don't wait to be inspired—you get inspired when it must be done, whatever it is.

We all think that writers or actors get inspired, and then go to work. It is the other way around. Whatever you have to do, get going and the inspiration will come.

So, there's no such thing as writers block. There's no such thing as waiting till everything is just perfect. There's no such thing as not being ready.

It's amazing what happens with you when you have a deadline. It gets done, doesn't it? Sure it does. You have to get it done, or else. How about setting deadlines for yourself? Tell a good friend what you plan to do and have them make you accountable.

I recently told a client of mine that I would reduce my fee by $100 every day I am late.

I used to be late. I'm not anymore. They used to be irritated when I was late. Not any more. I now get very inspired a few days before the 10th of every month. It's funny how that happens.

"In The Context Of Life's Circumstances, You Can Either Be The Victim . . . Or The Victor. The Choice Is Yours."

- Barbara Thompson -

Often times our expectations of people are higher than what they are capable of. We allow this to hurt us, to make us feel bad—disappointed. We desire that people treat us the way we would treat them—extend the same courtesies, be as thoughtful as we would be in the same circumstances. People are different. We can't allow other's actions and shortcomings to affect us so deeply—to hurt us so bad.

We can't always control what happens to us but we can control the effect we allow it to have on us. When the rug is pulled out from under us, we have to remain standing. We have to rise above and allow these things to empower us instead of devastating us—show that we are the better person. Maybe they will learn something from us.

15

"Joy Comes From Using Your Potential."

- Will Schultz -

What is your potential? What can you do if you thought you could do anything you put your mind too?

It's even joyful trying and not making it. You tried! Most people don't even try. They don't even get off the couch to give it a whirl. They are defeated in their mind without really even taking one step.

What do you dare to do? Do you want to be a writer? How about a movie star? Want to get married and have some kids? Start that business?

What thing do you want to do that gives you those butterflies? That's what you should be doing. Those butterflies are there to tell you that you're growing. They are there to remind you that joy is coming soon—whether it works out or not. They are there to remind you that you are going for your potential.

Try new things. Experience all the joy you can. There is no such thing as too much joy. Be joyful. Go for it. Be what you are destined to be. I know you can do it.

"Let Your Advance Worrying Become Advance Thinking And Planning."

- Winston Churchill -

Worry is a useless emotion. Worry in itself will not change a situation---action will.

At the moment you start to worry, make a list of all the tasks you can do to alleviate that worry. Take one of the tasks and do it at that moment. Maybe it's a phone call or a letter or going to visit with somebody. Do it immediately. As soon as you take that action, your worry dissipates. It dissipates because you have done something about it.

Use this in your business as well as your personal life.

17

"Nobody Can Give You Wiser Advice Than Yourself."

- Cicero -

This is so true. You know what you need to improve in your life. You might need someone to confirm it though. That is what counselors and mentors are for.

You know in your gut what is the right thing to do. You must learn to trust it. Some people learn to trust their intuition early in life and the rest of us learn later in life. As you get wiser, and you trust it and use it, and it's always right---you start to take your own advice.

I'd still ask for advice from trusted advisors, mentors and friends---the final decision should be weighed most heavily on your gut feeling. You know that. I'm not telling you anything new.

The next step is to put into action the advice we give ourselves. It's not easy. If we took all the advice we gave ourselves, most of us would be so much further ahead in our lives. I guess that's maturity. What used to take us 10 years to do, we can do in two years now.

"Overcoming The Unexpected And Discovering The Unknown Is What Ignites Our Spirit. It Is What Life Is All About."

- Daniel S. Goldin, NASA Administrator -

I can't imagine every day being the same. The unexpected is what is so exciting. You don't know whom you're going to meet today. You don't know what new thing you are going to learn today.

Being able to handle whatever is thrown in your way is also exciting. Knowing that whatever happens, you're going to be OK. It might take some time and experience to feel confident with this one. But, once you've been through a tough time and handled it, you add some confidence to your arsenal.

Life is such a beautiful experience. Part of that beautiful experience is not knowing what is going to cross your path. I'm sure you've had days that were just amazing. And at the beginning of that day you had no idea what was going to happen. If I were you, I'd walk around with that half-cocked smile waiting for that next great thing to happen in your life---because it will!

"Sooner Or Later Everyone Sits Down To A Banquet Of Consequences."

- Robert Louis Stevenson -

No act goes unnoticed in your life. Everything you do counts. All those little things add up. What are those consequences going to be?

Are you throwing things under the rug or are you dealing with them? It's easy today to NOT deal with them. It's easy NOT to take action today---to put it off till tomorrow. Doing that little task today that won't pay off for years is hard to do. Knowing that it might never payoff, might keep you from doing it ever. You have to do those things just for you today. Don't think about the outcome. Don't do them for the outcome.

Do all the right little things today, whether they ever pan out. They make you feel great about today. So do them today. Take the high road. Take the path not worn. Take it for you. Take it for the sake of taking it. And after a lifetime of doing the little RIGHT things---YOU'LL SIT DOWN TO A BANQUET FEAST OF GREAT CONSEQUENCES!

20

"Sow An Act...Reap Habit; Sow A Habit...Reap A Character; Sow A Character...Reap A Destiny."

- George Dana Boardman -

WOW! This is good. How much can I add? Well, here it goes: It's all about a little act. Something as small as an act can turn into your destiny. This is not going to take a weekend to accomplish--this is a lifelong practice. If you know that small acts can lead you to your destiny, you might think twice about the acts you are committing today.

So, certain acts will lead to habits you develop over your lifetime. What habits do you want to develop? Write down a list. It might be your health habits, your family habits, your spiritual habits, your business habits and so on. Start with little acts to create the habits you want.

By determining the habits you want to develop you have the foundation for the kind of character you want. And all your character traits determine your destiny. What is your destiny? You probably don't know what that is. That's ok, you will find it. Every little thing you do determines what your destiny will be--that's pretty deep. Take heed!

"The Greatest Weakness Of Most Humans Is Their Hesitancy To Tell Others How Much They Love Them While They're Still Alive."

- O.A.Battista -

Why is that? Are we embarrassed? Are we afraid? What is it? Why don't we do it?

I started a while ago. I went through a divorce and wasn't able to see my two kids every day. So, every time I talked to them on the phone and every time I saw them, I told them I loved them. It was easy for me to tell my children.

It wasn't as easy to tell my Mom and Dad, but I started around that same time. It's great to know that the last time you saw someone you loved that you told them you loved them. Who knows if it's the last time you'll ever see them. You don't really know. So, if you've said, "I love you," you can feel good about your relationship.

If you didn't say, "I love you" that last time, it's OK. Say it now. That person is listening to you. Go to their gravesite and talk to them. Write them a letter and tell them how you feel about them. They know you love them.

Now that you've been through this, start telling everyone you love, that you love him or her. It'll feel funny at first and then it'll feel great. "I love you!"

"Failure is the seed of success. You must have setbacks and failure if you're ever going to make it in this world. Talk to anybody who's successful and they'll tell you about the road blocks in their life."

- Anonymous -

I remember the first time I had one of my businesses go bankrupt (I've had 3 of them). I couldn't get off the couch. Finally after two weeks I figured that I better get out there and get going again.

I went to see Lou Bivonia. He ran a local insurance agency in my town. Lou went on to tell me of all the failures he had in his life and how he overcame them.

He then told me about some local business people I knew and what they went through. I felt relived. I thought I was the only one. Lou told me that I should wear my bankruptcy as a badge of courage. I do now. I'm not ashamed to tell those who are struggling about my challenges in hope that they will be motivated by them.

I know now that you must experience the setbacks or you will never be successful. And I'm so glad they happened to me early in my career. They still happen, but they're not big ones anymore. I can see them coming a mile away now.

You must be patient. For some, success comes quickly. For others, it takes a lifetime.

Remember this: you are on a journey. Life is a journey of learning. Look at those failures as classroom study. Learn from them. Don't do them again. And when you take your final test... you'll get 100%. I know you will!

"Failure is the seed of success. You must have setbacks and failure if you're ever going to make it in this world. Talk to anybody who's successful and they'll tell you about the road blocks in their life."

- Unkown -

You must be patient. For some, success comes quickly. For others, it takes a lifetime.

Remember this: you are on a journey. Life is a journey of learning. Look at those failures as classroom study. Learn from them. Don't do them again. And when you take your final test... you'll get 100%. I know you will!

"The More Reasons You Have For Achieving Your Goal, The More Determined You Will Become."

- Brian Tracy -

Get lots of reasons why you should achieve your goal. If you have many reasons you'll have to do it. You will have no choice.

Start small. Don't go after a huge goal right off the bat. Pick a reachable, achievable one first and go accomplish it. Now your confidence is strong. It's time now to after the bigger ones.

What is your goal? Write it out as if you've already achieved it. For example: "I weigh 120 pounds." The next step is reason and the benefits of achieving your goal: "fit into those jeans, better health, feel more alive, etc." Next, list the possible obstacles: "food, no time to exercise, negative thoughts, etc." List next what people and organizations can help you. And last, determine the specific skills and knowledge you'll need to acquire to help you accomplish your goals.

Do this simple exercise and you'll amaze yourself.

"We Act As Though Comfort And Luxury Were The Chief Requirements Of Life, When All That We Need To Make Us Really Happy Is Something To Be Enthusiastic About."

- Charles Kingsley -

Isn't that true? What makes you really happy? Is it that new car? It does for a while and then it wears off, doesn't it?

You and I need something that gets us up in the morning without the alarm clock. You can decide what that'll be. You need to set some goals and be working towards them on a daily basis.

I'm excited about writing one of these quote lessons everyday and hopefully it turns into a book deal. As I'm writing this, I don't have a book deal yet. I keep writing. This is the 158th lesson I've written. It's exciting to write whether or not it happens. I can't believe all the stuff that comes out of me.

What is your passion? What do you love to do? What is effortless for you? Set some goals in those areas and get to work on them. So what if they don't get you anywhere. It's the journey that's joyful.

Start right now and watch what that enthusiasm does to you!

"We Don't Receive Wisdom; We Must Discover It For Ourselves After A Journey That No One Can Take For Us Or Spare Us."

- Marcel Proust -

Have you noticed that as you get older that certain things you did when you were young disgust you now? Maybe you made fun of some other kids. Maybe you used to have temper tantrums. Maybe you were a wise-ass.

Cringing now when you think of those things is wisdom. You've learned over the years that those behaviors are not kind and loving. They don't make you feel good. Being kind and nice makes you feel good.

When I was young my parents protected me to a certain point. They let me fail and fall on my face all on my own. They let me experience ridicule from the other kids. They let me get a job and pay my own bills at an early age. You can't teach the lessons you learn from these things. You can only experience them—and experiencing them is wisdom.

The journey of life is your own. What you learn from it is up to you. You can treat each experience--positive or negative--as a lesson. Those lessons are your wisdom.

"Work Like You Don't Need The Money, Love Like You've Never Been Hurt And Dance Like You Do When Nobody's Watching."

- Anonymous -

WOW! This says it all! This is what we should all live by. Why don't you and I do this? You need the money. You've been hurt one to many times. You don't think you're a good dancer.

What this is really saying is that you should be your authentic self. Be like a little kid. When you were a little kid, you didn't know how the world expected you to act, so you were just being. Then, a little later on when you still acted like a little kid, your parents (or your teachers or anyone old) told you were acting like a little kid. You interpreted that as everything a little kid did, you should not. There should have been a disclaimer! One that said it's OK to act like a kid with most things.

Your work should be effortless. It should be something that you are so good at, and so enjoyable, that it's hard to separate your work from fun. I know that's a lot to swallow. There are people that have work like that. How did they do it? They tried a bunch of things and followed their heart until it brought them to their dream career or business.

You've been hurt. I've been hurt. Everyone has been hurt. There is no guarantee that you won't get hurt again. Don't look at those experiences as hurt, look at them as lessons. You got something great out of every hurt—cherish that. Give it up to the universe. The right person will present himself or herself to you.

Dance like you would by yourself. This is a hard one for me. There have been a couple of times in my life where I didn't care. I've kind of taken a new attitude about dancing and other activities like that: make believe that you are in a foreign country all the time and nobody knows you. If nobody knows you, you can make a crazy fool out of yourself and no one knows the difference.

Be who you are. You are a beautiful person.

"Your outer world tends to be a reflection of your inner world."

- Brian Tracy -

It definitely is!!

What you think about all day long is what you are or what you will become. Think about something as simple as where you are living now. You thought about it first, right? Now you are living there.

So you can think yourself to where ever you want to be in your life. Change your life on the inside and it will show up on the outside.

It seems simple. It is not. Changing your thoughts is not an easy task. You have to change the way you've been thinking for a long time. It is not impossible. Start thinking very doable things you can accomplish first. Train your mind that if it thinks about something… it will show up.

The next step is to start thinking about the big changes you want to make in your life. See it in vivid color in your mind. Daydream about it. Think about it day and night. If you do this--I promise you that the beautiful things you see for you in your mind, will become a reality!

"All Things Are Difficult Before They Are Easy."

- Thomas Fuller -

Do you remember the first time you rode your bike? I do. We started first on the lawn so that when you fell (and you did), you didn't get hurt. I remember that big, bright smile on your face when you came riding down our street for the very first time.

When you were four years old, riding your bike was the most difficult thing you ever did in your life. You don't even think twice when you hop on a bike now. It's easy now. It's effortless now.

Everything starts out very uncomfortable. It takes many efforts and mistakes to make it comfortable.

When you were younger, you were expected to walk, expected to ride your bike, and you were expected to read. Your mother and I knew you could do it. We also both know that you can do whatever you decide you want to do.

If you know that everything new you do is difficult first before it becomes easy, then you know not to give up at the first few mistakes. In fact, don't you give up till you accomplish it. I have faith in you!

"As I Grow Older, I Pay Less Attention To What Men Say. I Just Watch What They Do."

- Andrew Carnegie -

Do what you say you're gonna do. Don't say one thing and do another. If you make a commitment—follow through no matter what—even if you don't want to. You want to be known as the one who always does what he/she says. You want people to be able to count on you.

You will find out very quickly the kind of person he is by his actions, not by his words. And if he doesn't follow through with the little things—he definitely won't with the bigger things either.

Be careful to commit, because you must follow through. You'll learn this after a few (I really don't want to do this) commitments. Lead by example, not with your words and always do what you say you're going to do—NO MATTER WHAT!

31

"Do As Much As You Can, For As Many As You Can, As Fast As You Can And Someday Someone May Do Something Nice For You."

- Hugh Rundle -

Hugh hit it right on the nose with this belief. Why not help as many people as you can? How do you feel when you help someone out? You feel great! So why not feel great every day with your acts of kindness.

As fast as you can… that's a new twist I've never heard of. It makes sense though. When you act with speed, people consider you a person they can count on and trust. And if they can count on you, you'll get asked to do or join things that will benefit you in your life.

Someday someone may do something nice for you… Hugh is not expecting much in return, which is the way to handle this. You should give without expecting anything in return. The dichotomy is that you will get lots in return. You can't expect it, but it will all return for you in excess.

Everyone should have a "Hugh" in his or her life. That person would be a blessing for you. Why don't you become the "Hugh" in many people's lives? Enjoy the journey!

"Judging Others Is Ignorance."

- Gregory J. Colosi -

What right do you or I have to judge someone? We don't!!

When you judge someone you are judging a part of yourself that you don't like. You are really judging yourself. It's almost like looking in the mirror.

Are you making yourself feel better when you judge someone? What right do you have to say that someone is fat, ugly (These words are very uncomfortable for me to say. I'm saying them to get across a point.), short, tall, funny looking, a weird dancer or whatever you can come up with? People are all different, that is their beauty. The most judgmental people are the ones with the most insecurities. If you are secure with yourself, you'll accept and even learn to embrace people that are different from you.

How do you know what their heart is like? I've found that the most unique people that have been made fun of their whole lives, have become humble, non-judging, and sincere people. Those are the people you should hang with and aspire to be more like.

When you are young, you are starting to figure these kinds of things out. DO NOT JUDGE—ACCEPT! Individualism is so beautiful!

Most importantly, DO NOT JUDGE YOURSELF! Give yourself a break. You are going to make mistakes. You are going to make a fool out of yourself. You are going to say and do stupid things. You are going to really screw some things up. Forgive yourself, learn the lesson and move on.

33

"In The Middle Of Difficulty Lies Opportunity."

- Albert Einstein -

That goes for school, business and your personal life.

The difficulty was put there to teach you a lesson. It's up to you to figure it out. Are you gonna give up? Or are you gonna find a solution?

There is always a solution that is better than if you didn't have the difficulty. You'll say: "I wish this happened a long time ago."

Your best will be challenged and brought out during those difficult times in your life. You'll look back at those times as the stepping-stones in your life.

So… embrace the difficulties in your life—they bring the gift of opportunity!!

"Measure Your Wealth By What You'd Have Left If You Lost All Your Money."

- H. Jackson Brown -

Your real wealth has nothing to do with your assets. Let's take a look at what you might have left if all your money is gone.

The first thing I would think is your health. You might not think that's a big deal. Ask someone who is not healthy what he or she'd give to be healthy again. They'd give all their money—I bet.

Your family and friends: If you lose all of your money, you'll find out who your real friends are. They are the ones who care about you for who you are. They care about the loving and genuine person you are. They remember the fun and crazy times you had together. They remember when times were simple (and you had no money). A true friend is with you during the tough times as well as the good ones too. A really, really good friend steps up to the plate during those challenging times and sticks by your side and helps you make it through. If you end up with one or two of those kinds of friends during your lifetime, you've done well.

After all the money is gone, you still have you. You are a very powerful and determined young lady. You can make it through anything. It's part of who you are. Nothing is so difficult that you can't count on your Mom and I. You know you can always come to us for anything.

You are a very wealthy woman. You are very blessed.

"Nothing Is Impossible To A Willing Heart."

- John Haywood -

If you believe in your heart you can accomplish something, you can!

I'm going to take that a step further: If you thought of it, you can do it!

Your mind would have not let that idea into your head unless you could do it. So just the fact that you thought of it -- it's done!

So, think big thoughts. And then go after them. Don't ever let anyone tell you that you can't accomplish something. If you know in your heart you can -- you can!

Use that negative feedback as a positive force for action to help you accomplish your impossibilities.

I know you can do anything (and I mean anything) if you put your heart and soul into it. I have faith in you. Now you have faith in you.

"There is nothing stronger than love."

- Anonymous -

Love is the strongest elixir you can have in your emotional medicine chest.

You can use love to cure most anything that hurts your heart and your soul.

Love stands alone as the universal antidote.

Take love and use it to help others in need. Don't be afraid to use it. Don't be ashamed to use it.

A loving person will have the support of great friends and family.

If you act out of love, you are doing the right thing in every circumstance and every situation. Love is right!

"The great end in life is not knowledge, but action."

- Thomas Henry Huxley -

I know - you're in college. You're gaining all this knowledge and this guy, Thomas Henry Huxley is telling you that it's not the answer.

Knowledge is important. Action is more vital though. Let me put it this way: less knowledge with lots of action is better than lots of knowledge with little action.

Does that make sense?

Knowledge is useless without action. You can be the smartest person on the planet and if you do nothing with it, you're a waste.

You can only be a "C" student, but take lots of action and be a genius!

I hope I'm making sense. Don't get me wrong – I still expect "A's" over "C's". This is not to be used as an excuse if your grades slip. I hope you understand that.

This is hope for us non-geniuses. We can make it in this world if we're not. We just take lots of action. And if we fall down, we get up and take some more.

"The biggest risk in life you can take is taking no risks."

- Unkown -

Especially now! You are very young. You should be taking a risk every day. If you don't do something every day that scares the living daylights out of you ... you're not doing much.

The people that make it in life are the ones who fall on their face time and time again. Why? They're taking risks! When you take a risk and you don't make it, it's not failure. It might be a setback. Or a better way to look at it is that you found another way something won't work. Or you're getting closer to what works.

When you first starting walking (you were young, only 10 months), you fell. Did your mother and I say: "That's it, you're done. You had your try Courtney." NO! We kept it up till you started walking. That's what you gotta do. Keep at it till you make it. And that involves taking one risk after another.

"There Are People Who Have Every Reason In The World To Be Happy Who Aren't. There Are People With Genuine Problems Who Are. The Key To Happiness Is The Decision To Be Happy!

- Marianne Williamson -

You and only you decide if you're going to be happy. You can look at all the blessings in your life and decide that under any circumstance--you can be happy.

I'm not saying that you can't be sad for a day or two. You need to feel and experience sadness. You need to grieve sometimes.

When something bad happens to you--always remember this: There is someone out there who has had something worse happen to them and they are doing just fine.

If you focus on the positive aspects of your life, you'll be happy. You have so much to live for. We all do!

"Those Who Help Are Helped."

- Fortune Cookie -

Do you need help? Go help someone. Do you want forgiveness? Start forgiving. Do you want to be loved, start loving?

These are all very simple concepts. Actually, it's very selfish to help others. Why? Because, first of all, you'll feel great. And secondly, you'll be helped by those you are helping. It is a natural human thing to do.

There is so much joy in helping. You get to see and experience those beautiful smiles of those you are helping. You feel what they feel---the delight, the pleasure and the cheerfulness.

In the holiday season we all feel more like helping. Keep this feeling alive in you everyday. I know you can.

41

"Think you can, think you can't, either way you are right."

- Henry Ford -

This is so true. Read it again.

I'm a golfer. No more is this more evident than on the golf course. If you "know" in a 30 foot putt on the first hole, you feel like you can't miss. In the other direction, if you miss a 3 footer on the first hole, you are doomed for the rest of the eighteen holes.

We must teach our children this concept. Life success is made up in our mind. You can think your way to success. You can think your way to the gutter. You are a very powerful being. Think you can instead of thinking you can't. I know you can do it!

"Most People See What Is, And Never See What Can Be."

- Albert Einstein -

You have to make a habit of seeing what can be. It's the only way to live. It has to be as automatic as breathing for you. Always see the potential. There is always potential in even the most difficult and dreadful situations. It is your job to find it.

Be the one to see the joy in the joyless. Be the one to jump when jumping seems improbable. Be the one to sing when the others are sobbing. Be the one to smile when others are frowning. This attitude will get you much further in life.

You see the possible, not the impossible. There is always another road to take. Find it—it's there!

"She who would accomplish little must sacrifice little; she who would achieve much must sacrifice much."

- James Allen -

It's very simple; take it easy and your life won't amount to much – dare to sacrifice and risk, life will give you what you want.

This is as true as the sun rising in the east every day. It might not seem like the truth now, but it will when you get some experience under your belt.

Here's the key: YOU MUST NEVER GIVE UP!!

No matter what everyone is telling you, no matter how many times you have failed, no matter what your mind is telling you – YOU MUST NEVER GIVE UP!

You must keep going until you get what you want. The universe will give it to you. She is testing you. Your persistence and not giving up is your belief in yourself. The universe will reward that. There is no timetable though. You must keep going until... And the "until" might last a lot longer than you thought. This is where your real fortitude comes in.

Just know this: I believe in you! I know you will get what you want out of life.

"To Believe Your Own Thoughts, That Is Genius."

- Ralph Waldo Emerson -

You have genius thoughts. You always have. To believe them, that is the key.

Trust yourself. Trust your beliefs. Trust what you think up in your head. Trusting what you believe is genius.

I hope you can learn this young. For those that do, get ahead quicker in their lives.

You are an immensely powerful source of life and goodness. Believe in your own thoughts and you will see a miracle happen… the greatness of your own life!

"To The World You May Be One Person, But To One Person You May Be The World."

- Anonymous -

I'd like to know who said that! You never know who is looking up to you, admiring you. You are setting an example for someone.

It might be your little cousins (I know they do). It might be your schoolmates. It might be your friends. It even might be a teacher of yours. And even more far out--it might be one of your parents.

You are at the beginning of your life. Who are you setting the example for? The first person you should be setting it for is "you." That's right. Set the standards for yourself. They make you feel good when you do what you determine are the right things---don't they?

If you leave this world helping one person's life become easier, more loving, more positive, more uplifting or more of anything that makes them feel good---you are successful.

You've already helped many. Why not continue. You are such a beautiful person. Continue doing what you're doing. Put a little love into everything you do and watch the world around you become heaven on earth.

"We will either find a way or make one."

- Hannibal-Carthaginian General -

No matter what you want done in your life you can do. It's a matter of finding a way or making one.

I know you can do anything you choose. I know how you are. Don't limit yourself. If you think of it – you can do it!

Your mind is a very powerful tool. You can do anything you put it too.

Don't be concerned with the obstacles. They were put there for other people to give up on. If there were no obstacles, everybody would be doing it.

The obstacles test your belief in yourself and your ideas. There will always be road blocks in your way. They are there to make you stronger.

Nothing worth having in life is a walk in the park. You must struggle, dig, cajole and scrape your way to your dreams and goals.

I know you can do it! You know you can do it!

"No one is useless in the world who lightens the burden of it to anyone else."

- Charles Dickens -

What is your purpose in this lifetime? Maybe you don't know. Maybe you're one of the lucky ones who does know.

Your life does not go unnoticed to some people. If you've touched just one person in a special way in your lifetime you've done good.

Unfortunately, we don't always know who we've helped. Remember the teachers from grade school who made an impact on you? They don't know it. Not too many people tell their teachers how they helped them in their lives. Why don't you go tell those teachers in the next few days. Write them a letter, call them, or if they are still around, go see them. Tell them what you liked about them. Tell them how it's shaped your life.

If you're fortunate enough to have someone tell you how you've helped them, you're a very lucky person. It feels great to know that you've helped others. It gives you the ammunition to go out and help others. Start helping others and see how beautiful it is.

"First ask yourself: What is the worst that can happen? Then prepare to accept it. Then proceed to improve on the worst."

- Dale Carnegie -

Worry is a useless emotion! You'll live a longer and happier life if you don't worry.

The act of worrying has no positive effects.

Worry sucks the energy out of you. Instead of using that energy to worry, you should be using it to take steps to eliminate the worry.

When you find yourself worrying, make a list of the things you are worrying about. Prepare to accept the worst.

Next, write out the steps you are going to take and then take action immediately. Don't start tomorrow, start NOW!

This process will stop your worrying. Try it! I know it works. It works for me. Remember: Worry is a useless emotion.

"You Are Positive, Creative And Happy To The Degree To Which You Eliminate Negative Emotions From Your Life."

- Brian Tracy -

You must eliminate negative emotions from your life. You have to!

Your mind is like a garden. What do you plant in it? Are you planting positive thoughts or are you letting the negative weeds grow.

You must train yourself to think of the positive side of everything---especially the negative things in your life. Those negative circumstances are brought into your life to teach you. They are lessons. You will ALWAYS learn more from the difficult times in your life than you will from the easy times. You might not grasp the lesson right away---it will show up though---I guarantee it.

Part of these negative emotions that come in to your life are from the people you associate with. Try this little idea: only hang around with people you aspire to be more like in some way. You want the people in your life to be uplifting, positive, thoughtful, caring and all those good things. Why would you want to bring people or have people in your life that bring you down?

Get rid of your negative emotions by thinking positively and bringing uplifting people into your life. Start today and watch your little world be a happy little world.

"You can't fight love."

- Reinhardt Brucker -

You can't fight it! Love will always win. Love is the strongest motivator there is.

You can do anything with love. Look at what Gandhi did! He changed India without any violence. When the British beat his followers with gun butts and clubs they refused to fight back. Eventually the British gave up. They couldn't fight it. They couldn't fight love.

Try fighting for what you want with love. There is nothing for the others to fight against. They know you're doing it out of love and they want what you want.

About the author: Rein is a personal friend of mine. I met him in 1996. We spoke together for three months on the road. We clicked the minute we met. He is the kindest and most gentle man I know.

51

"A friend can tell you things you don't want to tell yourself."

- Frances Ward Weller -

A friend who can tell you things you can't tell yourself is a real, true friend. Hold on to him or her. It takes guts to tell you those things. Your friend is risking his friendship to help you.

My brother was asked by his best friend to be his best man in his wedding. My brother refused. He told him that if he was going to marry her, he would not. Today, Johnny is married to another woman-his soul mate- and has two beautiful girls. Twenty-five years later, they are still best friends. We all knew that the woman he was going to marry was not the right one for him. My brother was the only one who had the guts to tell him. And he was the only one.

"A Friend Is One Who Sees Through You And Still Enjoys The View."

- Wilma Askinas, Writer -

If you can leave this life with one or two people in your life that you can call a real friend, you've done well.

I learned a lesson early in my business career. I took a very successful business owner out for lunch a dozen or so times over the course of a two-year period. He was my business mentor at the time. We decided to do some business. He told me to contact his Vice President of Sales. I called him and told him that "my friend" (the mentor) suggested that I call him. We met and did some business.

Next time I had lunch with my mentor he gave me a lesson about what friendship is that I've never forgot. He explained to me what a friend was and that. I was not his friend. I was his acquaintance and someone he was helping out.

Friends, he told me were together through thick and thin for a long time. A friend is someone who calls you and sees you more when times are tough. A friend does not take advantage of you. A friend does not get jealous of you becoming successful and being happy. A friend does not talk behind your back. A friend knows every little secret about you and doesn't use it against you. You can call a really good friend and know before you call that they will do whatever it is you're asking---and they will do it out of love.

So every time the "friend" word is used, I remember Gene. Thank you for the lesson and God rest your soul.

"Always Think In Terms Of What The Other Person Wants."

- James Van Fleet -

Your first consideration should be how this "next act of yours" will affect the other person. The other person could be your spouse, your kids, your parents, your friends, your co-workers or someone you just met.

How will your friend react to what you are about to do? Always keep their feelings in mind. Always be considerate. Being considerate is one of the finest characteristics you can have as a human being. Being thoughtful is such a nice quality.

Think about your friends and family: are they thoughtful, considerate, selfless and giving? The ones that are like this are the ones you like the most---right? Take those qualities and model yourself after them. Notice how they react to certain situations and you do the same.

Opening the door, letting someone in line first at the supermarket, letting someone in traffic or just being nice and friendly is thinking of someone else before you. If you make a habit of doing this, your life will be full of joy and love---I promise!

"Determination And Perseverance Move The World; Thinking That Others Will Do It For You Is A Sure Way To Fail."

- Marva Collins -

You and only you will make it happen for you. Don't count on anyone else. You have your best interests in mind, nobody else does.

When you are young you have a tendency to wait for others to help you make things happen in your life. IT DOESN'T WORK LIKE THAT! If you want your life to go in a certain direction---you must step out of the pack and make it a reality.

You can do it! You have what it takes get out of life exactly what you want. There are people that will guide you, but not do it for you. Use them. They are all around you. You must seek them out. Sometimes they are hidden in books. Sometimes they'll cross your path exactly when you need them.

They are called teachers or mentors. When you are ready to learn the teacher will appear. You must recognize him or her though.And don't ever waste your teacher's lesson. If you waste your lesson, it is less likely that another teacher will show up next time when you need him.

You have been equipped with everything you need to make your life into whatever you want. You have determination. You have perseverance. You have the ability to never give up until you reach your goals.

Don't count on anybody but yourself to build your life. Nobody will come to your rescue. Nobody will be concerned about you like you will. I know you can do it. You do too.

"Use Every Letter You Write, Every Conversation You Have, Every Meeting You Attend To Express Your Fundamental Beliefs And Dreams. Affirm To Others The Vision Of The World You Want. You Are A Free, Immensely Powerful Source Of Life & Goodness. Affirm It! Spread It! Radiate It! Think Day And Night About It. And You Will See A Miracle Happen...The Greatness Of Your Own Life!"

- Author Unknown -

Is that powerful or what? We all hold back. Do you? I know I do sometimes. You gotta break loose and let everybody know what you're about.

What are you about? Do you know what you stand for? Are you a kid at heart? Are you loving and kind? Are you positive? Do you always look for the best in others? Are you fun? Are you happy? Are you emotional? Are you a hugger? Are you a smiler? (I just met this little girl--Miss Jane she is called--and she just never seems to stop smiling. It's so refreshing.) Are you a spontaneous dancer?

Starting right now, show everybody who you really are, especially the children. It's so easy to do with them. They don't judge us. They just go with it and give you their real feelings. Practice with the children and then move on to the adults.

Start being the person you really are. START RIGHT NOW!! You'll get some funny looks. You might even get some people talking about you. You'll start to stir some things up.

Those people judging you are wishing deep down inside that they too could be free and be themselves. They don't do it because of the fear of looking funny or crazy. They also don't want to be judged by others.

The heck with everybody else, be yourself. Be yourself to a fault. Be more of who you are. Get crazy! Get wild! Be you! Dance in the supermarket. Smile at everybody. Compliment strangers. Play with the kids. Say only nice things. Walk with a spark in your step. Let everyone in traffic. Make faces at little kids. Sing in the shower. Stop when kids are selling lemonade. Tell jokes. Be the first to say "hello." Stop and help people who's cars breakdown (did that last night). Wave at kids on school buses. Feed a stranger's expired parking meter. Live your life as an exclamation, not an explanation.

There's a start for you. Please, for yourself and for your own sanity, stop living a lie. Be exactly who you are. Express it every day. Some people won't like it--but the most important person to you will--YOU!

"To Me Success Can Only Be Achieved Through Repeated Failure and Introspection. In Fact, Success Represents 1% Of Your Work That Results From The 99% That Is Called Failure."

-Soichiro Honda, Founder, Honda Corporation -

I knew this was true, but I've never heard it said like this--and from someone who would really know. This puts a whole new spin on what you do in your life, doesn't it? If 99% of what you do is failure, then you shouldn't get disappointed when it happens, should you? Everything in life seems to be trial and error. Why is it this way? I think it's this way so that we can build character. And depending on what you go through, you build different levels of character.

Go talk to someone who seems to have it all going for him or her. Ask her about her life. You'll be surprised to find out all the hardships they've encountered. Early in my career I took a job selling life insurance after my business failed. I wasn't feeling too good. Lou, who ran the agency, was a very successful man. It seemed like everything that Lou touched turned to gold. I asked him about it. He told me about a bunch of failed business ventures he had in his career. He told me that life and business is about taking these so-called failures and learning from them. He also told me that they would keep coming and knowing how to handle them was the key to success.

Keep in mind that every successful person fails 99% of the time. We only see the successes. Go out and fail your way to success.

"Be Thankful For All Your Blessings. An Appreciative Person Makes A Pleasant And Optimistic Person."

- Brian Tracy -

Thanksgiving is a great time of the year to count your blessings. I have a blessings list. My list is composed of all the people in my life that I'm blessed to have around me.

When I get down, I'll check out my blessings list. I'll go through it and smile at each name and then I'll stop at one of them. I'll then get into more detail in my mind on how this person has affected my life. I think about the supportive things he has done for me over the years and how much he means to me.

Take a look at all the other blessings in your life besides your family and friends: your health, your career, and your community. And don't forget the little things: the crisp winter days, children laughing and playing, taking your dog for a walk, coming home to your husband or wife (or significant other), the smile of a stranger, the smell of coffee, the hugs of your friends, the great conversations, laughing, crying, talking about your loved ones who've passed.

You have so much to be thankful for. You are in a community of fabulous friends and family. You have it better than most. There is always someone or many someone's who are in a tougher place than you are. Pray for them right after you count your blessings.

Start today and smile at all the little blessings that come your way. Appreciate them and then spread them to others. That's how this blessings thing works. It is one your life duties--to spread the joy of blessings to everyone who crosses your path.

"The Most Basic Of All Human Needs Is The Need To Understand And Be Understood. The Best Way To Understand People Is To Listen To Them."

- Ralph Nichols -

Have you ever thought you knew why someone did something to later find out that you were way off the mark? It happens to me all the time. You and I don't know the inner workings of someone's mind and all the things they've gone through in their lifetime.

How could you know? You can't. From now on try not to judge or assume anything from anybody. You know what happens when you assume (look at these three words: ass--u & me)? And judging is just not right. You don't have the right to judge anyone for anything. I don't even like the word.

How do you understand where someone is coming from? Listen to them. Ask questions. And listen some more. Don't dominate the conversation. Just listen. Nod your head. Smile. Be compassionate. And just listen some more.

After listening, you should be able to understand where she is coming from. You don't have to agree--just understand. If you grew up in the same environment as she did and had the same life experiences that she did, you might think the way she does.

It's so nice not to judge (I can do it most of the time, but it's hard) and assume you know what's going on in someone's mind. You really need to hear their story. Everyone has his or her point of view.

If you seek to understand others, you will be understood. Listen, listen some more and then follow your heart.

Subscribe here if you'd like to get these life lessons every Friday. Please forward this blog to your friends and family.

"When An Old Person Dies, A Library Is Lost."

- Tommy Swann -

I had a friend (God rest his soul) named Cliff Wallace. I met him at age 90. He was at the tailor shop picking up a custom made suit. He had this big smile on his face and we struck up a nice conversation. As he was leaving, he told me that it was a "dividend" to know me.

I thought that was kind of unique. As he walked away from me, I was thinking, "I should get to know him. He knows something I don't." I ran after him and asked him to lunch. That was the beginning of a five-year relationship that lasted till he passed away at age 95. He still drove and played golf up until then.

We used to get together on Friday afternoons and have lunch about once a month. I learned many valuable lessons. Can you imagine if you could tap someone who's been through most of life's challenges and is still smiling? I had that opportunity. I'd ask him some simple questions like: "How do you stay in such good shape?" Or "I get mad when someone cuts me off in traffic. How do I stop that?" His answers were always "matter of fact" and simple.

I learned so much from Cliff. I still think of him and it's been fifteen years since he's been gone. I'm going to have to go back into my notes and see what other nuggets I can dig up. If you get a chance to befriend a mature happy adult--do it! You'll be all the wiser for it. I hope you are as blessed with this privilege as I was.

"I take nothing for granted. I now have only good days, or great days."

- Lance Armstrong -

"I'm having a bad day." I can't stand it when I hear that. Just the fact that you're alive makes it a good day, don't you think? When I think that things are going wrong, I always compare myself to others that are less fortunate. To them, the bad day I'm having is probably their dream day. So your worst day could be someone else's dream day. What do you think of that?

Let's take a look at a "so called" bad day and let's see if we can find the good in that day. Are you up for it? OK, let's get going.

You got up. You're alive and that's good. You have some breakfast. Millions don't get breakfast, lunch or even dinner. So your tummy is full. You get in your car. A car! You have a car. Do you know anyone who can't afford a car? I don't know any. You go to work or you own your own business or you take care of your kids today. So you have money coming in that takes care of your food and shelter. How many people in the world don't have that?

And that's not even the really good stuff yet. How about your family and friends who would do anything for you? Do you know how many people you affect positively with just being you? More than you think. I know that if you're reading this, you are special. You are special because you care about your fellow human beings.

Your lifetime homework on this subject: When someone tells you they are having a bad day, I want you to explain to them that their bad day is someone's dream day. Can you do that for me? One by one we'll get rid of the bad days.

61

"There is no revenge so complete as forgiveness."

- Anonymous -

Who benefits when you seek revenge? You might think you do, but you don't. Why? Because, you feel rotten afterwards. You might feel great immediately, but the long-term effect is rotten.

Why waste your energy getting revenge when the final effect on you is a feeling of distaste? I know why. It's because of how you and I are brought up. TV, movies, and the media all project revenge as the right thing to do when you want to get even.

If you seek revenge, he now thinks that he needs to get even and the vicious circle begins. This will never end unless one of you forgives or one of you dies. It's up to you to take the right course of action.

If you forgive, you will never have to waste your energy on getting revenge. Forgiveness is your revenge. You can now spend that saved energy on vital things in your life that will benefit you and your family.

Any energy spent doing things that are not good is wasted energy. Why waste your precious energy on doing not-so-good things? Spend it on good things.

So when someone does you wrong--FORGIVE HIM IMMEDIATELY! Feel sorry for him. Put yourself in his shoes. If you grew up the same way he did, in the same environment, you might act the same way he is acting. He acted that way because he knew no better.

Be the bigger one, take the high road and derail the "revenge train." You are a good person. You know this is the right thing to do. You might not realize it now, but it's better for your overall well-being.

Being a calm, understanding, generous, loving and forgiving person is the only way to lead your life.

"In Nature There Are Neither Rewards Nor Punishment--There Are Consequences."

- Robert G. Ingersoll -

It's that way in nature, why shouldn't it be that way for you? We get too caught up in success and failure. There are only results or consequences. Don't look at something as you failed--look at it as a result. OK, you tried it that way and the result wasn't what you wanted, so you try it another way.

And on the flip side, we also get caught up in our successes. I don't know about you, but my first major success went to my head (big time) and it ended up really screwing me up. If I looked at that as a consequence and not this big success, I would of been much further ahead.

I know it's hard, but you must keep an even keel about things that happen in your life. It almost has to be a non-event when you succeed or fail at something. It's just a result and you learn from that result. Hopefully you learn that that way of doing something is not going to work and you try something else. If you get it right the first time, don't think you have it together, cause you don't. Take it the same way when you don't get it right the first time--it's just a consequence.

Life is a series of lessons. How you respond to those lessons will determine the life you lead. Treating what happens to you as consequences will help you through life in a more positive and direct route.

"You Cannot Do A Kindness Too Soon, For You Never Know How Soon It Will Be Too Late"

– Ralph Waldo Emerson -

Be kind to everyone. Be kind in every situation. Why not? The not-so-kind would say that…"He really ticked me off. I should get back at him." Why? That it so childlike--so asinine. Why is so hard to just accept people for who they are and forgive them instantly if they do you wrong?

You have no idea how your kindness will help. And you might say, "Well, how's that gonna help me?" What goes around comes around. Whatever you send in to the universe will come back. And besides all that--IT MAKES YOU FEEL GREAT!!

You should treat everyone (with no exception) like it's their last day. Try this experiment: for the next 24 hours be as kind as you can be. Smile at everyone. Say nice things to everyone. Do nice things for everyone. Be the nicest, kindest, person you can possibly be for the next day.

I promise you this: your eyes and heart will open up to what life is really about. It is such a great feeling to always being loving and kind. It's such a simple way to change your life. Changing your life is not done with momentous changes--it's done with the little everyday changes.

I hope you will take my challenge--not for me, but for you. You wouldn't be getting this lesson unless you were the kind of person that is already doing this or headed in this direction. So, get on with it. I wish I could be there watching.

"Give your best to others and don't be surprised when they give their best back to you."

- Jimmy D. Brown -

I was talking to my friend John today in Starbucks and he asked what I was going to write about this week. I recited the quote and then I thought… "I think that John and I have this give-your-best-to-others thing working."

I call John the "muffin man." Most every Saturday John has a muffin for me. I feel a little funny taking it. But then he gives me a funny look, smiles, and gives me some butter to spread on it, so I take it.

I've been thinking about that in regards to today's quote. Whenever I have some extra soup, I tell John to stop over and pick it up, as I did today. I like giving it to him because he always tells me how good it was when I see him next.

And the vicious cycle continues…John gives me another muffin, shares some valuable computer technical stuff with me and I give him some more soup. When is this ever gonna stop? I hope never. I have a good thing going and I think John would agree with me.

I'm sure you have someone in your life like John. I'm fortunate to have a bunch of "John's" in my life. I have a number of dry cleaning customers of mine who are such great people. I don't mind if I have to jump through a few hoops for them to get something done. Actually, it's easy, no matter what it is.

The first step in this process is giving your best to others. Some won't return the favor and that's OK. They don't know about this concept yet. Just keep giving them your best even if it's hard to do. One day they might wake up.

Your best might just be a bright smile. It might be a nice greeting. It might be a compliment-you get the idea. Create a cycle that hopefully never stops--GIVE YOUR BEST TO OTHERS NO MATTER WHAT AND WATCH WHAT HAPPENS!

65

"Educated People Never Graduate."

- Bumper Sticker -

College* is only the beginning of your education. If you're smart (and I know you are), you'll get doctorate after doctorate in the study of life. There are so many things to learn. If you stop learning after college, you'll be a failure. I know these are harsh words, but they are true. Some of your education will come from classes like you're taking now and some will hit you right "between the eyes" when you least expect it.

When you get your first full-time job after college, you'll have to learn new information--not for a grade, but for your survival. If you don't learn what you're supposed to, you'll get fired. Your boss won't say, "You got a D," she'll say, "We have to let you go."

And in most cases, there is no curriculum. You'll have to design your own. You have to figure out what you need to learn to survive and prosper and then go design your own self-study course. Unfortunately, most of your really valuable learning will come through setbacks and challenging situations. The key is not to react to it right away, even though you'll be hurting with lots of emotional pain. Let it settle in for a couple of days and ask yourself: "what did I, or can I learn from this situation." In the months and years to come, you'll smile from what you learned.

There is so much to learn about life. And once you learn one thing, there are so many more things to learn. You'll never exhaust the new courses you can take. And the most exciting thing is that you decide what courses to add to your curriculum. There will be no grades, just consequences.

Educated people commit to life-long learning. "What did I learn today," is a question you should ask yourself every day for the rest of your life.

*Written for my daughter Courtney while she was in college.

"He who is good at excuses is generally good for nothing else."

- Samuel Foote -

Don't make excuses! It is your fault-- good or bad. Weak people make excuses. A strong person never makes excuses. There is always a reason you can think up that will justify in your mind why you didn't do something.

Winners never make excuses, only wieners do. Are you a winner or a wiener? You can choose at this very moment. Commit to never making an excuse again. How can you do that? You can start from this instant to take full responsibility for your life and everything that happens in it.

I take this excuse thing a little further that I should. If someone runs a red light and they hit me, I think it's my fault. I know you might not agree. I should have looked before I took off. If I did, I would have not been hit. I know this is a little extreme, but I'm such a fan of the "no excuse" policy.

You can smell a wiener a mile away. Stay away from them like you would the plague. If you let them in your life, you'll start to make excuses too. Deciding on and following through with the "no excuse" policy will turn you into a fully functioning human being who makes things happen in your life. Take full responsibility for everything that happens--good or bad. Make no excuses--just make things happen!

"An ounce of action is worth a ton of theory."

- Friedrich Engels -

Theory or talk is worthless. A person is not measured by what they say they're going to do, but by what they actually do. Talk is cheap.

I know talk is cheap from experience. I used to say, "I'm going to do this" and "I'm going to do that," and my 7-year old son Ryan taught me that talk is cheap. He said to me, "Dad, you don't do what you say you're going to do."

I said (stunned), "What do you mean?" "Last weekend you said we were going to see the X-Man movie and we didn't go." And then he went on to tell me of all the other things I said I would do, but didn't. I was shocked at all the promises I made and didn't follow through with. I committed at that moment to never do that to him again. And I never have and it's been twelve years.

My son taught me to never promise anything that I won't do. I've promised a lot less since then and I've done a lot more--in all areas of my life. That's not to say that I don't slip up once in a while (never with him though).

And because of this lesson my son taught me, I see this flaw clearly in other people. Some people promise the moon and give you very little or nothing. In business, this flaw will eventually put you out of business. You have to give what you promise. In business, it's a good idea to give more than you promise--actually over DELIVERING is the best. And I guess that goes for life too.

Become a person of action, not words. Thank you Ryan! I love you.

"Life Promises Us Sorrow. It's Up To Us To Create The Joy."

- Opti the Mystic -

Written for my daughter Courtney…

Nobody goes looking for sorrow--it just finds us. I believe that the man upstairs wouldn't give us anything that we couldn't handle. LIFE IS A TEST OF CHARACTER. The more setbacks and sorrow you have, the stronger your character will be.

I know it's hard to think of it that way--especially when you're in the middle of it--but it's true. Good comes out of sorrow. It strips down life to what really matters to you. It clears your mind to what is really important.

I can tell you this: it's not the nice cars, the big house, the nice clothes, or the great vacations. It's people who matter in your life. You matter in my life. Your brother matters in my life. Grandpa and Grandma matter in my life. Your Uncles and Aunt matter in my life. My other family members matter in my life. My close friends matter in my life.

So how do you create your joy? It's pretty easy. First of all, stay close to those that you love. Spend time with your family and close friends. Don't waste it watching TV. Focus on activities in your life that make you happy. You are young; it's easier for you to get started now. Do those things in life that you really like. You have a clean slate.

I have always worked toward professions that make me happy. That's why sometimes it seemed as if I was going backwards. Monetarily, I might have been, but spiritually I was going forward. I quit speaking when you were 11 because I didn't want to be traveling all over the country so I could be home watching you cheerleading.

You can also find joy in life's little moments. I was having coffee yesterday making faces at a cute little red-headed girl. That made me feel good. You are a very positive and joyous person. Take time and find joy in everything you do. I love you!

"In Nature There Are Neither Rewards Nor Punishment--There Are Consequences."

- Robert G. Ingersoll -

It's that way in nature, why shouldn't it be that way for you? We get to caught up in success and failure. There are only results or consequences. Don't look at something as you failed--look at it as a result. OK, you tried it that way and the result wasn't what you wanted, so you try it another way.

And on the flip side, we also get caught up in our successes. I don't know about you, but my first major success went to my head (big time) and it ended up really screwing me up. If I looked at that as a consequence and not this big success, I would of been much further ahead.

I know it's hard, but you must keep an even keel about things that happen in your life. It almost has to be a non-event when you succeed or fail at something. It's just a result and you learn from that result. Hopefully you learn that that way of doing something is not going to work and you try something else. If you get it right the first time, don't think you have it together, cause you don't. Take it the same way when you don't get it right the first time--it's just a consequence.

Life is a series of lessons. How you respond to those lessons will determine the life you lead. Treating what happens to you as consequences will help you through life in a more positive and direct route.

"When you blame others, you give up your power to change."

- Robert Anthony, Educator -

When you don't get it done, it's your fault. If you do get it done, it's your fault. It's such a simple concept. It's ALWAYS your fault!

No matter what happens in your life, you are responsible. There is no one else or no other circumstance you can blame. If you go through life with that belief, you'll be very successful.

When you blame someone or something, you give up your power to change. When the blame is somewhere else, you can't change it. You don't have control over any circumstance or any person. The only thing you have control over in your life is YOU! You can blame all you want, but it all comes down to YOU! No matter what happens to you, you are to blame. Am I getting the point across? I hope so. This is such an important concept in life.

So many people blame the weather, their boss, their parents… their everything. They are drowning in self-pity. GET UP! Take responsibility, and get going with your life. When you decide to take life at face value and know that you are responsible for everything that happens to you, you make your life a beautiful masterpiece that you create.

Don't wait for anyone or anything to change. You must do the changing. If you have a challenge or setback, you are the only one who can take care of it. You are the only one who can turn it around.

Take the "bull by the horns" and make your life everything you want it to be. It can be whatever you want--YOU DECIDE!

71

“The greatest obstacle to discovery is not ignorance --it is the illusion of knowledge.”

- Daniel J. Boorstin -

The more I know, the more I realize how much I don’t know. Don’t kid yourself into believing that you are intelligent. If you are, be humble about it. There is always something new to learn.

Don’t be a “know-it-all.” Nobody likes them. They seem to know all the trivial facts about everything except for what really matters. If they knew what really mattered, they wouldn’t be shooting their mouth off about knowing something about every subject.

Always favor the side of not knowing. Nobody is an expert about everything. If you don’t know much about a subject--keep your mouth shut! Discuss only those subjects that you have a deep interest in and know about. And in those subjects, you still don’t know everything.

Look at even the subjects you know a lot about as only the “tip of the iceberg” about that subject. You can always learn more about it. The greatest thing about knowledge is that you can always gain more knowledge. You are never done. You never know everything about a subject. You can always learn more.

One last thing: never seem to know what someone is going through unless you have gone through it yourself. Even then, you still might not understand.

Always understate your intelligence. Don’t shoot off your mouth. Learn something new everyday. Stay humble about subjects you know lots about.

"In Youth We Learn, In Age We Understand."

- Marie von Edner-Eschenbach -

Written for my daughter Courtney when she was in college.

You do learn a lot when you are young. Most of it goes in one ear and out the other. You can't help it, you're young and don't know any better. Some of that learning is stored in the depths of your brain and comes out when you are ready to use it.

Your Grandfather always told me to "work from my neck up." When I first heard it, I said to myself, "yeah, yeah." It didn't really sink in. Today, my whole adult business life is based on that! I won't enter any business if that is not the case. I am striving every day to only work that way. I don't know if Grandpa knows how much of an impact that has had on me.

Now I have the chance to do that with you. Your Mother and I have pounded good manners and lessons into you and Ryan from the day you were born. We have always hoped that they have sunk in. I'm very proud to say that they have.

Attention young parents: IT DOES WORK! You might be thinking that you teach them the right things to do and they just don't listen. DON'T GIVE UP! Keep teaching them. They are listening. It's just the way it is. Our kids pack it away till they really need it. And unfortunately, it's not until they are older. It really starts to show up after they have left the nest and start to fly on their own. Oh… it feels so good to see your hard work come to fruition.

It feels so good to see you grow into the woman you are. I am so proud of you and all that you are. I love you!!

"Never Take The Advice Of Someone Who Has Not Had Your Kind Of Trouble."

- Sidney J. Harris -

When you really think about it, why would you take advice from someone who's never been through what you're about to go through? It makes no sense at all, but we do it all the time. Just because someone is older, is a relative, or makes lots of money-- doesn't give them the right to give you advice on something they know nothing about.

You've all had that brother-in-law who knows everything about everything or the friend who's a "know it all." Whatever you do, don't take advice from them on anything. Let me take that back. Just do the opposite of everything they tell you and you'll probably be doing the right thing.

When I was starting my first business I went out and sought the help of a very successful businessman. His company does over a billion dollars today. He gave me some priceless business advice--advice I could have never found in any book. It came from his own personal business experience. I still remember and act on the critical things he taught me. He also told me not to take advice from him on being married. He told me he was no good at it. I respected him for that. He is a very wise man, only dispensing knowledge on the things he was good at.

So from now on, only seek knowledge from those who know. How do you find out? Ask him or her what their experience is with that particular subject. If they say they don't have any, don't take their secondhand advice. Only take firsthand advice from people in the know.

"If You're Never Scared Or Embarrassed Or Hurt, It Means You Never Take Any Chances."

- Julia Sorel -

Go out today and get scared. When is the last time you left your comfort zone? You should do it at least once every couple of days. When you're in the zone, you should do it everyday. Say what's floating around in your head to the person who you want to say it to. Don't let the moment pass. Bypass your fear and spit it out. You'll feel great after you do. I do this all the time with compliments. I compliment strangers. If I see something I like, I tell them. It could be a child, a beautiful woman, or a senior citizen. I get it out and it feels great.

Go out today and get embarrassed. Go out on a limb. Do or say something that you would have never said before. Let that blood flow to your face. Let everyone see that you're vulnerable and that you can get embarrassed. It's a different feeling. It's humbling. It builds character.

Go out today and get hurt. If you take chances, you will get hurt emotionally. If you play it safe, you'll never get hurt, but you'll never experience real joy either. There are always two sides to the coin. Take an emotional chance and you'll get hurt or you'll feel ecstasy.

Getting scared, embarrassed and hurt are all good things. They might not seem like it initially, but they are. This is what life is made out of. Go enjoy your life and do what scares, embarrasses, and can possibly hurt you.

"The Most Important Thing in Life is to See to it That You are Never Beaten."

- Andre Malraux -

This doesn't mean that you get beat playing golf. This means that you never give up. You have control over that and no one else does. No one can beat you unless you give him or her permission--and you never do. Never, ever give up. You can call it a day, but you never throw in the towel.

You can stop doing something a certain way and try it another way--that is not being beaten. You can close one business and go start another one--that is not being beaten. You can get rejected 37 times with your book proposal--as long as you keep writing, you're not beaten. I'm sure you get the drift of what I'm talking about here. Basically I'm saying that you should never, ever give up on your dream.

It doesn't matter how old you are, never give in and declare yourself beaten. No matter what happens to you, you must stay and fight. Life has a funny way of only sending you disappointments that you can handle. Just knowing that should give you the strength to handle it. Those who give up don't understand this "Life Law." They may get a few roadblocks in their way and then it's Quitsville.

Don't be a quitter. Be a winner. How do you do that? By never giving in. I know you can do it and sooner or later you will too.

"Kindness is more important than wisdom, and the recognition of this is the beginning of wisdom."

- Theodore Issac Rubin -

A message for my daughter Courtney two weeks before she graduated from college.

Wow! This is a good one. Wisdom has nothing to do with intelligence. I know intelligent people who can't get out of their own way. Wisdom is one of those things that you can't have when you're a twenty-one-year old unless something profound has happened in your life.

I once saw a twelve-year-old boy giving an interview on TV. He had cancer and the prospects of him living too much longer were not good. He spoke with so much caring and love in his statements. This boy had to grow up fast. The serenity than engulfed him was angelic. He spoke from his heart with so much wisdom. He knew things that most forty-year-olds don't know. This boy had wisdom.

Most of us don't go through that much in our lives at such a young age. Wisdom comes with experiencing life's up and downs. Unfortunately, most of our wisdom comes from the down times in our life.

So, how do you get wisdom? Everyone has the same chance. It has to do with the way you evaluate what happens to you in your life. When something goes wrong in your life, how do you look at it? Do you say, "poor me," or do you look for the lesson? If you want to become wise, you look for the lesson. And there are lessons everywhere, if you look for them. You will find them in the strangest places.

Start being kind to everyone. Make your first thought, a thought of kindness when you are dealing with people and situations. You will be amazed what happens. I don't want to tell you, you have to experience it on your own.I love you!

"The Purpose Of Life Is To Fight Maturity."

- Dick Werthimer -

My 19-year old soon accused me the other day of having the mentality of a 3-year old. I must be fighting maturity.

OK--you must be mature about some things, but for the things you don't have to--you shouldn't.

You shouldn't be mature about forgiving. Little kids don't even know what not forgiving is because they do it automatically. They never hold a grudge. They don't know what that is until they are taught.

You shouldn't be mature about judging. Kids don't judge. They make friends with whoever is around. They don't care what kind of house their new little friend is living in. They don't care what color their little friend's skin is. They only care about the person.

You shouldn't be mature about how you act. Little kids act from their heart. They do what comes naturally to them. They know no different. Have you ever just sat and watched some kids go about their little lives? It is amazing. I watch with astonishment and awe!! I wish I could be more childlike!

So here's your assignment: Act like a kid. Do a Chinese fire drill. Make faces at little kids. Sing and dance (while sitting) in your car. Ride a cart at the grocery store. Whistle to yourself. Talk with everybody. Smile at everybody for no reason (I was in the grocery store yesterday and this beautiful little toehead around the age of one was just smiling from ear to ear at me. I couldn't help but smile. That little moment made me so happy.) Be goofy! Do things at the spur of the moment. You know what I'm talking about. Do whatever a kid would do.

I'm sure you've heard the old saying that "youth is wasted on the young." Now you have a chance to recoup your youth on a daily basis--GO OUT STARTING TODAY AND ACT AS JUVENILE AS YOU CAN!!

"Happiness consists not in having much, but in being content with little."

- Anonymous -

Most young people think that a big house, expensive car, and lots of money will bring them to nirvana. It's not true. Don't get me wrong, those things are nice, but they won't bring you happiness. In fact, if you're not happy, those material things will bury your happiness so far that you might never be able to find it again.

So what does make you happy? I know what makes me happy. I just got done with a walk with my wife this morning. The sun was shining and the birds were chirping. Its springtime and all the flowers and trees are starting to bloom. The smells are so euphoric and the fresh air is so grand. That little fifteen-minute walk made me happy.

I'm going to make a new gnocchi dish with butternut squash this weekend. That makes me happy. My daughter is graduating from college tomorrow. That makes me very, very happy-- on many levels. She starts her full-time-after-college job on Tuesday. That makes me ecstatic.

Going to garage and estate sales makes me happy. Using my silver (which I bought at a garage sales for $12) at every meal makes me very happy. Actually, the things I paid the least for make me the happiest; not only for the joy they give me but also because of the low price I paid for them.

Going to coffee with my friends makes me happy. Playing golf with my father, brothers and nephews makes me very happy. Playing bocce with my buddies makes me very happy. Sitting on a bench and watching everybody and everything makes me happy. Starting up conversations with complete strangers makes me happy.

Getting up in the morning and being able to write this makes me very, very, happy. I guess that there's not too much that doesn't make me happy. Can't write any more. Gotta go play golf with my Dad. Happy Days!

"[Have You Ever Had] The Kind Of Morning That Lasts All Afternoon."

- John Mayer, from his song "Why Georgia" -

Had you ever had a morning like that? I bet you have. Why can't all or most of our mornings be like that? You don't have to wait for some time in the future for this to happen. You can have those mornings right now. It all starts with you. It's your perception of what a beautiful morning is.

You don't have to be on the ocean or on vacation for this beautiful morning thing to happen. It can happen right where you are now. It can happen wherever you live. It can happen in a small apartment or a big house. It's not where you are physically--it's where you are mentally. Where do you want to be mentally every morning? You can turn everyday ordinary mornings into magic by changing your frame of mind.

You can also have a great night that lasts all morning. Think about it? You can have a day that's so fantastic that it lasts a week. You can have a week that is so fulfilling that it lasts a month. You can have a month that is so overwhelming beautiful that is lasts a year. And you can have a year that was so good to you that it lasts the rest of your lifetime.

And even if you've had some challenging times--when you look back--those times of struggle end up being the best years. Get rid of those bad days. I can't remember having a bad day. All my days are varying levels of great days. It's all how you perceive what is around you. It's all there for you in your life right now to make this morning, this night, this day, this week, this month, this year and this lifetime the greatest it can possibly be for you.

“Everybody thinks of changing humanity, but nobody thinks of changing himself.”

- Leo Tolstoy -

Especially when you’re young, you think you can change humanity. YOU CAN’T CHANGE HUMANITY!

The only way you can affect others is by changing yourself. And that happens very slowly. If you start to change yourself, others you are associated with will change to. They will change by absorbing some of who you are because they are in their presence.

I like being positive all the time, even when I’m not, as you can probably tell. So when I leave someone either in person or on the phone, I say, “Make it a great day.” Most people say, “Have a great day.” I added a little more positive-ness to it for my liking.

I ran into Dawn the other day, who used to work for me over fifteen years ago. She was with some of her girlfriends. After some introductions, one of her friends said, “Isn’t Greg the one who started the ‘make it a great day’ thing?” Dawn told them that I was the guilty one. I didn’t even know I had an effect on Dawn. And now fifteen years later some of my positive influence is still there.

I know that you become like the people you hang around most of the time. Hang around the right people and on the flip side, these are the people you have the most influence over. And those people will start to influence those around them. And the circle of influence begins.

You can start to change humanity--although a little slower that you might of wanted--by changing yourself first. Your influence will help her change herself. Your influence will help him change himself. Go out and be the best person you can be--that’s the best you can do to change humanity.

"It is the reaching out with love to help another which is important....not the results. Reach out with love...that's all you need to do."

- Excerpted From A Course In Miracles -

Love is the best action you can take in any situation. Acting out of love is the only way to act. What the person you are reaching out to does with that loving action is up to them. You are not responsible for that. You are only responsible for always acting out of love.

Acting out of love all the time is not easy. There are times when someone will lash out at you and your quick response is to protect yourself in a negative way. That's normal for most people.

Let's try it another way. Suppose you knew why he was lashing out at you. You could read his mind and that day he lost his job and he didn't know how he was going to support his family. How would you react then? I'm sure you'd show some compassion. From now on I want you to make believe you know what's going on in people's lives.

Maybe she just lost someone she loved. Maybe she just got swindled out of a lot of money. Maybe her husband just left her. I'd like you to look at every lasher as though something negative is going on in their life. Her lashing is a way of looking for love. She just wants someone to understand what she's going through. If you practice this mentality, you'll get really good at acting out of love in every situation.

If you always act out of love you are doing the right thing in any given situation. YOU MUST LEARN TO GET OUT OF YOUR OWN WAY AND NOT THINK OF YOUR OWN FEELINGS! It's the feelings of the ones you're spreading love to that counts.

"Every person born in this world represents something new, something that never existed before, something original and unique"

- Martin Buber (1878-1965) -

You are unique. It is something to celebrate. Usually the unique and different people are the ones who find success much quicker than the rest of us. They know who they are early in their lives. It is obvious to the rest of us who they are because they don't hide from it.

You must find that uniqueness about you and bring it out in full force. Don't keep it from the rest of us. And most importantly, don't keep it from yourself. Please don't hide from it because you are embarrassed. You shouldn't care what other people think. I know this is a hard concept to grasp at your age, but you must be you at all costs. You will learn over time not to let the opinions of others bother you.

You must find joy in those individuals who are different and aren't afraid to show it. They are true to themselves. They know they beat to another drum. They know the world looks at them in a funny way.

If you are in search of the real you, you must find out who you are. You must always be on the lookout for when you show up. When you do, you must embrace it and let you be free. Finding out who you are is a big part of your spiritual growth. I want you to be exactly who you are. In fact, I will encourage you to be more of who you are. Do this for your friends too. Let them be the person they are. Encourage them to be like it all the time, even when they're not with you. Your friendship will grow and deepen.

You are a beautiful and unique woman. I'm so lucky to have you as my daughter. I love you.

"Keep True To The Dreams Of Thy Youth"

- Johann von Schiller -

I can't stop thinking about my dreams--can you? I used to think I was crazy, but I'm not. I've met people who have accomplished incredible things and they still dream their dreams.

Why should we stop? We shouldn't. Who says that at a certain age that you can't dream anymore? Your dreams might change over the years, but there are still some from your youth.

I have a dream list in my planner. OK, now you know. It's out of the bag. I'm a dreamer! I used to teach "dream listing" many years ago in a management training company my brother and I had. We had people list everything they wanted to be, have and do.

What would be on your list? Do you want to travel somewhere? What do you really want to do for a living? Writing was on my dream list and I'm doing it at this very moment. Do you want to paint? Do you want to run in a marathon? Do you want to adopt a child? Do you want to write a book? Do you want to lose some weight? Do want to be an actor? Do you want to direct a movie? Do you want to start your own company? Take 5 minutes and write out everything you want to be, have and do. If it pops into your head, you can make it a reality.

Don't abandon your dreams. They are a part of you. Don't ever listen to the naysayer. Listen to the dreamers. Be a dream weaver (that's a song, isn't it?). Encourage those around you to go after their dreams. DREAM ON BABY!!

"By the time a man realizes that maybe his father was right, he usually has a son who thinks he's wrong. "

- Charles Wadsworth -

The older I get, the smarter my father gets. When I was 18, I was brilliant and my Dad was stupid. I knew everything about everything. Nobody could tell me any different. I'm 49 years old now and I don't even know what I don't know.

The things my Dad told me all these years are starting to make sense. My 19-year-old son thinks I'm a dummy, but I think he's smarter than I was at his age. There is so much wisdom that you can get from your father. I'm lucky, I have a great one.

I guess the most wisdom I can gain from my father is following his example. I think this is the best way you can share what you know with your children. I never heard a negative word from my father towards me or my siblings (and that goes for my mother too). I only heard encouragement.

I was forty-two when I heard my father swear for the first time, and I've never heard another one since. I asked him why he didn't swear and he told me that he never heard his father swear. I don't swear too much and I hope my son learns this lesson too.

The wisdom eventually sinks in. Fathers, your children will get what you're telling them. It might take 40+ years, but they'll get it. Don't give up. It works!

Special Consideration: Please say a prayer for my Dad. He's in the hospital and we don't know what's wrong yet. It's been 13 months since they removed his cancerous tumor and he was doing great. Let's pray he'll be OK again. Thank you!

"Life may not be the party we hoped for, but while we are here we might as well dance."

- Anonymous 83 year-old woman -

Life usually doesn't turn out how we hoped it would, even for Tiger Woods. I'm sure it didn't turn out how he liked. He probably never thought he couldn't go to the grocery store, movies, or out for dinner, without being mobbed. I'm sure he'd love to be like everyone else when it comes to these simple pleasures.

I'm sure Tiger finds his simple pleasures in other areas. What are your simple pleasures--the things you dance for everyday? I use my good stuff everyday. To me, everyday is a special occasion. I use my Mont Blanc pen everyday. I don't save it for those special days when I can show it off. I show it off to myself everyday. It feels so good using it knowing that it's such a great pen. It was a gift from a good friend of mine and I was going to wait until my first book signing. I wear my best cologne everyday. I wear my best shirts all the time, even with jeans. I have steak and eggs with a filet, not a cheaper piece of meat. Why not?

Why save the best stuff for the special days. Today is a special day. Today is the day to celebrate. You have no other day. Tomorrow might never come. A lot of people say they will travel when they retire. Hogwash! Travel now. If you like traveling, travel every chance you get. They don't have to be exotic trips, it might just be a day trip to somewhere you've never been or somewhere special. Remember, we don't save special for special days.

Celebrate today. Don't put off the joyous things in your life. Do them now. Tell those you love, that you love them. Don't sweep anything under the carpet. Tell those you love how you feel everyday. Life should be celebrated everyday. Find the joy in the simple things. Find the joy in the everyday things. Find joy in everyone you meet. I hope you can do this. There is even joy in some things you might find unpleasant. Discover your life and celebrate the moments of it.

"Life Is What Happens To You While You're Busy Making Other Plans"

- John Lenin, "Beautiful Boy" -

Sometimes when you are so intense at going after what you think you want in life, you miss the boat. Have you ever rushed to get somewhere and you forgot to bring something. You were just worried about getting there and you forgot why you were going.

Life is sometimes like that. We rush everyday to get to work. We rush at work to get things done. We rush home. We rush to get dinner and get our kids to bed. We are so focused on getting everything done that we miss life's simple pleasures.

STOP!! Right now I want you to look out your window. What do you see? I see the shadow that a tree branch is making on the house next to me. The sun is sneaking through the trees and making it's way to the ground. I'm just looking at it in marvel.It's so beautiful. Do you see any birds? How about some squirrels? Or just a bee buzzing around? Go out and walk in the grass barefoot. Do you feel the texture of the grass on the bottom of your feet? I bet you're smiling now.

When you're friend comes over to talk, stop everything that you're doing and give her your full attention. Stop your mind from thinking of what you've got to do next. Just be! Be there in that moment. Soak up all that moment has to offer.Relax and feel the peace come over you because you are feeling that moment. That moment if what life is all about.

Life is a series of moments like that. They can be here everyday. You decide if you want to take advantage of it. I was with my friend Mike yesterday. We played golf in Canada. The traffic was very slow as we were crossing the Rainbow bridge through customs.Guess what Mike did? He got out of my car and walked on the sidewalk soaking up all that the falls had to offer. It was night and the red, white and blue lights were gleaming. He could feel the mist and I bet the smells added to the experience. Mike is a "moment seizer." What everyday things in your life can you turn into experiences that will last a lifetime?

I think we all ought to be more like Mike and enjoy our moments--what do you think?

87

"If you act out of love, you'll always make the right decision."

- Gregory J. Colosi -

I know it's my quote. I had to write about it because I believe it's so important in our lives. It doesn't matter what the decision is--put love in the equation and it's the right decision.

I'm not talking about just any love. I'm talking about unconditional-get-your-ego-out-of-the-way love. If you can look at the decision you are about to make and tell yourself with care and concern that you are making this decision based on love--then it's the right decision.

I dare you to challenge me. You can't. Think about it. Try to come up with an example that including love in your decision won't make it the right decision. It's not gonna happen. Making a decision based on unconditional love will always be the right decision. I don't often use "always", but in this case I am. This is how strong I feel about using love in your decision making process.

Using greed or non-love in your decision-making processes will always backfire on you. Initially it will seem like it works, but eventually it will not. You'll take a couple of steps forward and then later on you'll lose ten steps.

Use the factor of love in all of your decisions and watch your life blossom. Take the high road in all the decisions you make using "love-based thinking."

"Facing it, always facing it, that is the way to get through. Face it."

- Joseph Conrad -

Sweeping it under the carpet is not the way to handle the challenges you have in your life. For most of us, it is our first thought. It's easier for a while because we make believe it's not there. But as it sits there, it's growing. And the longer we let it sit there the bigger and bigger it gets.

Some people are very natural at facing all that goes on in their lives. When you analyze it, it really is better to face it head on and don't let up till it's solved. When you let it go, you don't really let it go. You think about all the consequences of not taking action. You think of all that might happen, most of it is nonsense. So you really go through much more pain just letting it sit and doing nothing about it.

I have found that once you take action, the fear of facing it goes away--even if it's the worst possible scenario. Now you can focus your energies, not on worrying, but on getting the challenge solved. It's a much better feeling to be working on the known, not the unknown. You seem to have more energy this way.

You and I both know this is the way to tackle any and every challenge in life. During some periods we pull back for whatever reason. Just knowing this can help you move ahead and make your life what it should be.

"I always turn to the sports pages first, which record people's accomplishments.

The front page has nothing but man's failures."

- Earl Warren -

When I was 18, I read a book called the "Magic of Thinking Big," by David Schwartz. In that book he told me that I should never watch or listen to the news and not read those parts of the newspaper that were negative. I'm 49 and I haven't (for the most part)!

Why fill your mind with negatives that are not a part of your life? Schwartz went on the say that those things that affect you in the news will be read by someone close to you and they will tell you. So you don't have to fill your mind with all that negative stuff for no reason.

Some people I've encountered think I'm a "Pollyanna.". I say, "So what!" Is living a "Pollyanna" life that bad? I don't think so. Pollyanna's are always happy and content. What's wrong with that? Anyway, my head is not in the sand; I know what's going on. I happen to focus on the just the positive stuff in my life.

Amazingly, I've run into other people like me. There are tons of them in certain pockets of society. Actually, they are everywhere. I choose to hang out with them because they have a positive, can-do attitude all the time. I'd rather be with them than the negative, can't-do people. What group are you going to hang out with? Whatever choice you make will determine the kind of life you will have: an optimistic one or a pessimistic one.

Oh, and one more thing. You can spot (and feel) the negative ones a mile away. They've always got something terrible to say and they suck the energy right out of you. You know the type. I'd run from them, like you'd run from a burning house.

"When People Talk, Listen Completely. Most People Never Listen."

- Ernest Hemingway -

This is such an important skill. And a very hard one to conquer.

Try to listen and not think of what you want to say next. This is very difficult. If you're thinking of what you want to say, you aren't listening to a thing they are saying. Try listening without responding. If you do that, you can listen completely.

Have you ever had a conversation with someone and they are always cutting you off. It's annoying. I used to be like that. Now I wait till they are done talking and count to three--and then I respond. Try it. It takes some practice.

You can be a great conversationalist by just listening and nodding your head once in a while.

And I've found (being a male) when talking to a woman who has some challenges--just listen and don't (I repeat: don't) come up with solutions. We as men want to fix things. Women want to talk it out and be heard.

Listening is a great skill to have. I've talked too much. I have to go.

"If I had to live my life again, I'd make the same mistakes, only sooner."

- Tallulah Bankhead -

Wow! This is a good one! And it is so true. The people who get ahead the fastest in life are the ones who make the most mistakes. It's the only way you learn. You don't learn much from your successes--it's the failures that really give you the schooling.

Once you make lots of mistakes, you know how to handle most situations. And when that situation comes up again, you'll know how to react to it. I was just talking to a friend the other day about some of the mistakes she used to make with people. She'd make friends with anybody who was willing to make friends with her. Most of these people were a drain on her because she had her act together and she was a great listener. Since then she has got rid of those who sucked her energy and only kept those who give her energy. Now she won't accept a friend (it sounds a little cold and calculated, but it's not--it's for your own good) unless that person has positive energy. She told me that she's been fooled a few times, but she's getting better at it.

So what mistakes can you make ASAP to help you through life: someone getting hired when you thought you had the job all locked up, getting in a fender bender (oh, you already did that one), picking the wrong boyfriend or spouse, getting fired from your job (I got fired from my own company), buying the wrong car, taking the wrong job, picking the wrong business partners (it's most difficult to pick the right ones), saying something hurtful to the person you love (you really can't take it back), buying a piece of real estate only listening to the realtor without doing your own investigation, picking a profession solely based on how much money you will make, not telling a person you love how you feel about them before they die (so you should constantly tell them how you feel about them), holding in your emotions (let them go), etc. I can't think of all of them, you'll just have to go through it.

When you boil down life, it's a series of joys and mistakes. Knowing that the mistakes will bring you more joy from the lessons is one of the greatest secrets of a successful life. Go out and make those mistakes! The sooner you do, the more life will happen.

"Life is not measured by the number of breaths we take, but by the moments that take our breath away."

- Anonymous -

Some people go through life just taking breaths. They get up every day and do the same thing over and over again without thinking about their life.

Someone asked me the other day what my favorite day was. After thinking about it for a moment, I told her that I didn't have a favorite day and went on to say that I couldn't single out one day as my favorite because every day was exciting to me.

You've got to look for those "take-your-breath-away" moments in your life. Once you think about it, you can find them everywhere, everyday. I love the fall. You can find natures beauty glowing in the trees, even the smells of fall take your breath away. The crunching of the leaves sounds great too. Every season has it take-your-breath-away moments.

Be aware of what's around you. Babies take my breath away. They are so honest with who and what they are. They do exactly what they want, when they want to. I saw a friend of mine playing with his daughter Gabriella in the leaves the other day. That made me smile and bring a tear to my eye thinking of you (I'm glassy eyed right now just thinking about it). That was a take-your-breath-away moment for me. Look for life's little joyous moments; they are all around you. You've just got to notice them.

If you have a chance to do something you've always wanted to do--DO IT!! Don't think of the reasons you shouldn't. Come up with the reasons you should. Life is meant to be enjoyed. So go find the joy. Do what makes you happy! Do what knocks-your-socks-off! You should be laughing your butt off every day.

Don't be happy with the status quo. It's up to you (and only you) to create your own joy. Do things that take your breath away. Be with people that take your breath away. Create a life that takes your breath away. I love you.

"Others are merely mirrors of you. You cannot love or hate something about another person unless it reflects to you something you love or hate about yourself."

- Anonymous -

This really takes some thinking about. I've thought about this concept long and hard over the years and have found it to be so very true. What you say about others is what you're really saying about yourself. You wouldn't know what you like or dislike about someone else unless you've experienced it yourself.

When you show restraint saying something negative about someone else, you've been there yourself and you know that's not a good place to be. When you still lash out, you still have that negative trait and you don't like it and that's why you see it in someone else. If you didn't have that trait, it wouldn't bother you that that person has it. So if you're still lashing out, you need to work on yourself in that area.

Now my favorite part--something you love about someone else. Those kind and loving traits you notice in others are the traits you have or are working on developing in yourself. I'd say all the kind words you can about someone else because they reflect well on you.

So when you comment about someone else, you are really commenting about yourself. Be careful what you say because the words coming out of your mouth, no matter whom you direct them at, are directed at you. My mother taught me to keep my mouth shut unless I have something good to say. I think she knew something.

"There Is More Credit And Satisfaction In Being A First-Rate Truck Driver Than A Tenth-Rate Executive."

- B.C. Forbes -

This is so true. Be proud of any job or business you have if you are giving it all you have. I often thank the garbagemen (no women yet) for the job they are doing. I tell them that I really appreciate them and what they do, and I really, really do!!

Some kids are not "cool" with what their Mom and Dad do for a living. It doesn't matter if they're sweeping floors or they are a rocket scientist--you should be proud of your parents for providing a nice home and environment for you to live in. And you parents--give your kids a break. If they decide they want to wait on tables, encourage them to be the best they can be. Being the best they can be will transfer to when they find their passion (and if it's still waiting on tables, you still can be very proud of them). It's their life, not yours. I have a friend that told her parents to get used to it--"I'm gonna be a waitress. I enjoy it."

Maria Shriver, in her book, had 10 principles she lived by. One of them was that no job was beneath her. That is so important. A friend of mine went from a high level executive with the New York Post to shoveling sidewalks to pay for her rent. She did it in style though--in her full length fox fur coat. If you gotta mop floors to get by, YOU DO IT!! Get your ego out of the way and be the best mopper you can be. It doesn't matter what anyone thinks and who cares anyway--it's your life.

I have a friend who knocks on doors to sell his product. You could put that in the category of a vacuum cleaner salesman or a Fuller brush man. My friend makes over a half million dollars a year.

I am so turned on by people who have jobs or businesses that are "beneath" the so called "cool" people. They are so in tuned with who they are and what their purpose is.

I have so many more examples of people who are into their jobs. It doesn't matter what you do--DO IT WELL, GIVE IT EVERYTHING YOU'VE GOT AND BE PROUD OF IT!

95

"Commit A Random Act Of Kindness."

- Bumper Sticker -

What happens when you are kind to someone? Don't you feel better? Actually, I think it's selfish to commit acts of kindness because it makes you feel so much better. This is one time that selfishness is good (and there are a few more).

When is the last time you really went out of your way to be kind to someone? I want you to look for it. You'll feel some butterflies when you find it. That is the sign that you should commit your act of kindness.

A couple of weeks ago, a beautiful smiling female senior citizen, working at the gas station, slammed her finger in the cash register waiting on the person in front of me. When I got up there, I asked her which finger she hurt. She showed me her baby finger. I took it and kissed it! She had this smile on her face that gleamed of joy. She told me that was the nicest thing that's happened to her in months. I made her feel great and selfishly I felt great too.

Go commit an act of kindness today.

96

"Every Good Thought You Think Is Contributing Its Share To The Ultimate Result Of Your Life."

- Grenville Kleiser -

Written for my Daughter Courtney

You are what you think about all day long. You thought about going to college, and here you are. Your thoughts are very powerful. You can think yourself into any situation you want in your life.

Everything you've ever done first started as a thought. You thought you could ride your bike, you did! You thought you could be a cheerleader, you did! You (and your squad) thought you could be in the nationals, you did!

As you can see, you are where you are today because of your thoughts. Don't stop thinking of where you can be. Nobody can stop you. Draw strength on the challenges you will face. When it gets tough (and it will), you get tougher.

It's a game. Those who do not give up---win! It's that simple. Give up and you lose. Keep going and you win!

Think you can... think you can't, either way you are right. I know you can be anything that you want in life. You have already proved that. I will support you in whatever you want to do. I am here. Use me.

I love you.

"Don't be too timid and squeamish about your actions. All life is an experiment."

- Ralph Waldo Emerson -

Life is an experiment. You are going to make mistakes. You are going to fall on your face. If you don't take a chance--where are you? What have you accomplished? Nothing. You've learned to not risk. If you don't risk, you've failed. If you risk, and it doesn't go the way you planned, you haven't failed. You've learned something new. Something that will come in handy later in life.

I want you to take chances. I want you to go for it. I want you to leave your comfort zone everyday. If you don't, you're not growing as a person. You are standing still. Nothing is absolute. There are no guarantees. Nothing is definite. It's kind of fun not knowing what the result is going to be--don't you think? Life is a big experiment. The ones who experiment the most are the ones who lead the fullest life. Hiding behind a rock will make you old before your time. Always taking the safe route in life will lead to a dull and unfulfilled life leading to nowhere.

Move forward with confidence. You will get better at making the right choices. There will always be times where it's a crap shoot. Roll those dice and see how your life unfolds.

98

“Life is not important except in the impact it has on other lives.”

- Jackie Robinson -

I believe that we are put on this earth for a purpose. And that purpose is to effect and impact others in some positive way with your gifts. What are your gifts? What were you put on this earth for? It doesn't have to be some grand scheme. It can be as simple as to raise a child or to be a good brother, sister, daughter, son, spouse, or whatever.

Maybe you won't find out the impact you've had on others until the final days of your life. It's not about you! It's about all those people that are in your life. Yes, you've got to take care of yourself, but not be selfish about it. Selfish people are not helping anybody, not even themselves. It might seem like it, but in the end they get no benefits from it. They end up alone and who wants to be alone?

How good does it feel to help someone out? It feels real good!! There is such a natural high from always being in the helping mode. It is the sure way to happiness. How can you not be happy helping others? You can't!

"Do Definite Good; First Of All To Yourself, Then To Definite Persons."

- John Lancaster Spalding -

We always forget ourselves. That is the person we should take the best care of. If you take great care of yourself, you'll better be able to take care of those important to you.

Being good and doing good is what life is all about. Why would you want to do badly? When you treat others badly, you feel bad. Why make yourself feel bad on purpose? Take the GOOD ROAD! Traveling on the "good road" is exciting, joyous and fun. You'd be amazed at the people you meet and the things that happen to you on the "good road" in your life.

Make sure the people in your life that matter, know it. Do good for them all the time. Even if they don't appreciate it now--they will in the future. If you have a child, you know what I mean.

Spread your "good" whenever possible. If you have a chance to do "good," DO IT! If you have a chance to compliment someone, DO IT! If you have a chance to do a favor for someone, DO IT! If you have a chance to smile at someone, DO IT! And most importantly, when you have a chance to do something "good" for yourself, definitely DO IT!

Be a "good spreader" down the "good road" in your life. Enjoy the journey!

100

"Be Happy For This Moment. This Moment Is Your Life."

- from the movie Unfaithful -

This moment is your life. Are there any other moments? No there aren't. You (and I) must live each and every moment of every day. Who knows when it will end. I don't. Do you? Of course you don't.

So what kinds of things do you think you and I should do? I've got some ideas. Want to hear them? I thought you would. For starters, I think you should wake up happy if you're alive. If you wake up and you can breathe, there is reason to celebrate another day of wonderment in your life.

Make time for visiting with the people that matter in your life--and even the ones you just met. Is your time better spent watching TV or visiting with friends? I was in Cuba recently and they only have two TV stations and not much in the way of professional entertainment. So what do they do with their time? They go down to the street corner and talk. You see them all smiling, laughing, getting serious and waving their hands all over the place. That is their entertainment. We used to do that. Where has it gone? I believe that you can make a conscious effort to bring that back into your life. I have.

If you have a chance to go on a trip--GO ON IT! If you have a chance to spend a day with a friend--DO IT! If there is an opportunity to compliment someone--GO FOR IT! There are so many things you can do every day to live in the moment. You will know when the opportunities pop up. Take those times and LIVE IN THE MOMENT. That moment is what life is all about. You'll be much happier and you'll bring someone (or many) along with you. Have a blast and go for it!!

Made in the USA
Charleston, SC
18 January 2011